A Weekend
to Change Your Life

ALSO BY JOAN ANDERSON:

A Year by the Sea: Thoughts of an Unfinished Woman

An Unfinished Marriage

A Walk on the Beach:
Tales of Wisdom from an Unconventional Woman

A Weekend to Change Your Life

FIND YOUR AUTHENTIC SELF

AFTER A LIFETIME OF BEING

ALL THINGS TO ALL PEOPLE

Joan Anderson

BROADWAY BOOKS · NEW YORK

BROADWAY

PRINTED IN THE UNITED STATES OF AMERICA

BROADWAY BOOKS and its logo, a letter B bisected on the diagonal,
are trademarks of Random House, Inc.

Visit our Web site at www.broadwaybooks.com

First edition published 2006

Book design by Gretchen Achilles

Library of Congress Cataloging-in-Publication Data

Anderson, Joan, 1943–
A weekend to change your life : find your authentic self after a lifetime
of being all things to all people / Joan Anderson.—1st ed.
            p.   cm.
    1. Women—Psychology. 2. Women—Conduct of life.
        3. Self-realization in women. I. Title.

HQ1206.A63 2006
158.1082—dc22
2005054333

ISBN 0-7679-2054-6

3   5   7   9   10   8   6   4   2

To the weekend women who strive to grow and change.

May you become tomorrow's mentors.

Contents

Acknowledgments xv

A Note from the Author xix

Introduction 1

PRE-WEEKEND:
UNDERSTAND YOUR NEED FOR CHANGE

11

WAKE UP, SISTER. IT'S YOUR TURN   13

Recognize That You Are Lost   13

A Leap of Faith   19

Give Your Life the Focus It Deserves   22

The Cluttered Calendar   25

Calendar Control   28

    But *Versus* And   32

    Star Power   35

FRIDAY:

THE IMPORTANCE OF RETREAT

37

SELFHOOD BEGINS BY WALKING AWAY	39
An Argument for Solitude	39
Become a Scholar of Self and Soul	43
One Woman's Retreat	46
Courting Retreat—Starting Small	50
The Extended Retreat	56
Knowing Your Sense of Place	58
Things I Walked Away From	60

FRIDAY EVENING:

RETRIEVE YOUR RAW MATERIAL SELF

63

PUT YOURSELF BACK TOGETHER, PIECE BY PIECE	65
Sturdy Roots	65
The Black Sheep Leads the Flock	69
Make a New Creation Out of the Old Self	71
Relative Ability	73
The Camera Never Blinks	77
Life Cycle Logic	79

The Colors of Your Life 82

   Intentions 88

   Crazy Quilt 90

SATURDAY:

REPAIR BODY AND SOUL

91

TURN UP THE SILENCE, TURN DOWN
THE VOICES 93

   Seize Your Day 93

   Empty Out 100

   Lighten Your Load 101

   Serendipity 102

   Gifts from the Sea 106

   A Scavenger Hunt for Your Soul 114

   Navajo Vision Quest 116

   Quiet Time 119

   What I Found at the Beach 121

BODY AND SOUL 123

   Getting Physical 123

   To Thine Own Body Be True 127

   A New Perspective on High Maintenance 130

   The End of Body Bashing 135

Here's to Self-Care 137

Hot Tubbing and Skinny Dipping 140

Training Body and Soul 145

SUNDAY MORNING:

REGROUP BY FINDING BALANCE AND BOUNDARIES

147

SURRENDER EVERYONE ELSE'S EXPECTATIONS 149

Waking Up 149

Love Letters from the Sand 152

Performing a Balancing Act 157

What to Keep and What to Dump 166

Couponing 168

Give and Take Questionnaire 169

SUNDAY AFTERNOON:

REGENERATE BY EMBRACING YOUR SECOND JOURNEY

171

GATHER YOUR STRENGTHS AND
SPONSOR YOURSELF 173

Embark on Your Second Journey 173

A Second-Journey Poster Child 177

A Good Life Is the Best Revenge 180

We Are Our Choices 183

Never-Ending Crossroads—Multiple Choices 185

Being Bold 188

Small but Powerful Journeys 191

Second-Journey Questionnaire 195

Collecting Compliments 196

POST-RETREAT:

RETURN

199

DECIDE TO BE NEW IN AN OLD PLACE 201

Re-entry 201

Slow Down, Don't Move Too Fast 204

Secrets Are Power 207

Remaining Enlightened 209

Salty Sisters 211

Create Your Own Lifeline 215

Lifeline Steps 217

Be Generative 218

AFTERWORD: CONNECTING THE DOTS 223

A Jump-Start Agenda for a Weekend to
Change Your Life 235

Acknowledgments

Developing a self and changing my life all started with an original group of seekers from suburban New York: Cheryl Lindgren, Judy Greenberg, Hazel Kim, Joya Verde, and Virginia Dare. Thanks for agreeing to search for ourselves together. And then came the numerous weekend retreaters who returned to their homes (in some forty-nine states) and began to tell the story of change—by giving speeches, talking to a friend over a cup of coffee, at their book clubs, or by organizing a workshop to coincide with my visits. Together we have given birth to a new movement—"the unfinished woman" movement. To all of you I will be forever grateful.

In *Arizona*: Joyce Anne Longfellow, Sally Arnold, Bernice Grassel, Bunny Perkins, Yvonne Rojas, and Barbara Hoffnagle. In *California*: Susan Jeannero, Sylvia Bays, Charlotte Hollingsworth. In *Georgia*: Kathy Wheeler. In *Illinois*: The founders of Maggie's Place, Barbara Benson and Nancy Powers. In *Pennsylvania*: Barbara DeFlavis,

Martha Enck, Betsy Miraglia. In *Florida*: Julie Debs and Susan Pinder. In *Michigan*: Sue Ann Schredder, Dawn Shapiro, Char Firlik, Julie Morton, Tonja McCullough, Peggy DePersia, Linda Masselink. In *Minnesota*: Nancy Jorgenson. In *Massachusetts*: Sally Hunsdorfer. In *Nebraska*: Anna Anderson. In *Iowa*: Alice Book. In *Louisiana*: Vicki Armitage. In *New Jersey*: Cincy Cutcliff, Terry Maricondo, Elaine Ottoway, Kyle Sabitino, Cathy Cohen.

Special thanks to Jody Donohue for offering her ad agency to promote my work. Also to Pat Haney, who used her videotaping skills for some of my speeches, and to the Chatham Bars Inn, which gave me lodging when I needed to get away. Producing a book as well as a program takes a team. Stacy Creamer, my editor, believes strongly that women need a push to grow and change, and, as such, she has been a great supporter of the premise of my program; Liv Blumer, my agent, supported my voice as a memoirist, and now has gotten behind my new voice as a mentor; and my assistant, Debbie Ebersold, has been a wonderful conduit between me and the weekend women, holding the logistics of my weekends together while I was busy writing this book. My deepest gratitude goes to Rebecca Anderson, my advisor in all things editorial, who traveled with me to get the pulse of today's woman and then insisted on addressing issues that could make a real difference in the lives of women wanting and seeking change. And last but not least, to the Salty Sisters, a group of women who met over a weekend and continue to affect each others' lives via e-mail, regular visits, and vacation retreats. You are the proof of Margaret Mead's sentiment: "Never doubt that a small group of thoughtful, committed citizens can change the world; indeed, it is the only thing that ever has."

A Note from the Author

In this book, I draw on the voices and stories of many of the women I have met over the past nine years. Some examples are composites, some are drawn directly from my weekend workshops, and some are based on interviews I conducted for this book. In all cases I changed the names to protect the privacy of these women, who are still growing and changing.

Introduction

Most women in their thirties to their seventies are asking the same question: "How, after being all things to all people, can I become what I need to be for myself?"

"Impossible," I hear some of you saying. "It's just too much work."

"I could never unload enough of my obligations to address the question fully," say others.

Well, perhaps. But you see, I was once so emptied by answering to everyone else's needs and expectations that I was desperate. Simply showing up for life no longer sustained me. I knew that I needed to listen to my heart and start taking better care of myself. But, like you, I didn't know how. Then, one day, I took a leap of faith and ran away from home for a time. I have not looked back since.

My flight was a pure gut reaction. I was halfway to a hundred and I figured it was now or never—listen to my own voice or continue simply to follow the pack. Somewhere deep inside of me I knew there were myriad unheard longings, ideas, and plans that I had grown used to ignoring. It was time to set them free. Escape seemed to be the only answer. Going to a place where I could be alone—apart from friends, family, and outside influences—would help me start again, get back in touch with who I was and wanted to be.

Certainly there was a price to pay. My decision to move by myself to Cape Cod was really unpopular, if not downright threatening to most people in my life. Aside from one confused and angry husband, many friends and acquaintances called me selfish, while others concluded that I had simply turned into an aggressive feminist. I bristled at the abrasiveness of the latter label. Couldn't they see that I was simply at a turning point and in need of new direction? Still, their judgments fed my fears—it certainly seemed that I had lost all compassion, and was even going a bit crazy. All I knew for sure was that I was tired and empty. The soft side of me had been buried by a culture that insists we *do* rather than *be,* and I didn't much enjoy the life I was leading.

After a year spent alone, trekking through the dunes and hiking along the beaches of Cape Cod, I gradually gained some clarity, reconnected with my intuition and instinct, repaired the wounds of self-neglect, and uncovered a fresh slate upon which to design the rest of my life. Along the way, I realized that the barbed labels cast my way had very little to do with me. They reflected everyone else's fear of change and of not being able to lean on me. My job was to save the only life I could save—my own!

During my year alone, I was fortunate enough to meet a wise old woman who became my friend and mentor. Joan Erikson was married to the famous psychoanalyst Erik Erikson and had collaborated with him on the theory that one's identity is formed through an eight-stage life cycle. In addition to her work with her husband, she was an artist, a listener, and a seeker. She showed me how to dance beyond the breakers, to pick up the dropped stitches of my life, to live in the moment, to nourish and love my body, and to never stop embracing adventure. Her friendship sustained me during my difficult journey—she buoyed my flagging spirits with her laughter and love of song, she kept me company on particularly dark and lonely nights, and she helped me find a sense of purpose beyond my despair by encouraging me to be generative and share my experiences. I hold dear her most significant lesson, that "we all have a responsibility to help ourselves to whatever wisdom and support come our way, and then, most importantly, to pass it on."

So, when some old friends came to visit and noticed not only a new bounce in my step but my carefree, happy outlook, they declared that they wanted some for themselves, I looked back at the steps that had led to my transformation. Although I had felt my way through those first few months, simply allowing my days to happen rather than holding to clear goals and objectives, I did see a pattern to my experience and quite a few exercises that had helped to keep me moving forward. With Joan's encouragement, I chronicled my story in three best-selling memoirs, designed to encourage other women to step outside of their lives, if not for a year, then for a week or a weekend, to learn to listen to what their hearts need to tell them.

The books struck a nerve. Scores of women poured into bookstores for my appearances, others invited me to their book clubs, and it was increasingly impossible to keep up with all the letters and e-mails expressing their relief that someone had put their exact feelings into words. Everyone wanted more—more stories, more inspiration, and more direction. Two letters illustrate the point:

> *I just finished* A Walk on the Beach, *and I'm enthralled. At this point in my life, where everything I have known and done for the past twenty-seven years is ending and changing, I admire your courage to take hold of your own life. But how did you actually do all of this? Can you give me advice? Is there some sort of roadmap I should follow?*

> *I've just finished reading* A Year by the Sea. *Your book really touched me in many ways. I am fifty-two and at a time when I need to reinvent myself. The way you just packed up and went to the beach was wonderful but bewildering to me. I seem to be frozen in my space, and although I would like to move for a short time, forever is too scary.*

How did you get the courage? How did you live through the boredom? How did you get over the impatience? In your book it all appears to be simple and I know that it is not. What can I do?

Clearly, other women have the desire to find purpose beyond the roles that they play. All they need is the time, some supportive cheerleading, and some gentle guidance. So I began hosting Weekend by the Sea Retreats. Now, some eight years later, women continue to come from all over the country to these retreats, and to the workshops I conduct on the road. They come to learn how to uncover the selves they have papered over so thoroughly, year after year, decade after decade. They come to walk the beaches, share their stories, and, with the help of my hindsight, reconnect with their own true selves. They all come with *the ache* and point their fingers at stagnant marriages, demanding kids, newly empty nests, overbearing bosses and unchallenging careers, and, yes, most of all, at the way life has lost its luster. I greet them and say, "Welcome to the club, sister. It's time to get a new life!"

Who are these women? They are career woman who thought they could do it all; stay-at-home moms whose children have gone and left them craving a new purpose; newly widowed or divorced women facing lonely futures in a couples-driven world; young mothers who have escaped the demanding noise and activity of their lives for the first time;

single women who wonder if they have missed something by not getting married. Besides mothers, they are also daughters, sisters, aunts, grandmothers, and friends, who come from fifty states and Canada. They are both desperate and courageous—ready to do what it takes to become their own persons. During the retreat, they learn to be in the present, deviate from the path, unlearn the rules, indulge in time off, be perfect in their imperfections, and take action to force change.

Although truly walking away, even for a weekend, is a luxury for many of us, finding the time to change is a necessity. Yes, there are hurdles. But most of them are of our own making. When I was on *The Oprah Winfrey Show* and talked about leaving home in order to find myself, a woman in the front row raised her hand and insisted that she couldn't possibly do anything like that. "I have several children," she complained, "and a job and a husband."

I felt her confusion as well as her indignation about my story, but I caught my guilt, sat straight up, looked her in the eye, and asked: "There are eighty-seven hundred hours in a year. Doesn't it seem pitiful that you can't find twenty-four just for yourself?"

"Pitiful!" Oprah responded with her wonderful drawl. "Did you hear her? Pitiful!"

The audience roared with laughter, but long after the show concluded, I came to realize what an important point had been made. If women don't find time to regenerate and restore, it is indeed pitiful. In fact, I don't know one woman who can claim that her family insists she find twenty minutes of joy! What's more, no one pushes us toward freedom or escape. We have to reach out and grab it for ourselves. This reaching takes a tremendous amount of will and courage, but as Joan Erikson once said to me, "It's a weakness to just sit and wait for life to come to you."

We need not spend another moment being strangers in our skin. We've been good girls long enough. This book is meant to motivate you to get a new life. In it I offer you the steps I instinctively took during my year by the sea, as well as the process followed at my Weekend by the Sea Workshops, all the while mixing my story with the stories from other women.

It is not meant to be hard work or to have any time constraints connected to it. We women don't need more work, or anyone else telling us what to do. Besides, you can't put a time frame on soul work. There are as many routes back to self as there are women to take the journey, and ultimately, everyone must design her own path.

Some might prefer that their angst simply pass. They don't want to hear that it's time for them to take their turn, to pull themselves out from under all their roles, to overcome their years of ingrained stage-fright and step into the spotlight, to project their voices out as far as they can and shout: I want, I need, I *am.*

But it's not just the work that stops them. It's the lack of guidance. We all need more mentors. Our traditional systems of support have crumbled. Too many families are divided by divorce and separated by distance. Mothers and daughters rarely share the same points of reference, values, or expectations. So many of us feel isolated and adrift. In this book, as I mix my story with the stories of other women retreaters, I hope you will begin to feel at home with our needs and our process and to find a network of support.

This is not a conventional how-to book. I can't stand how-to books, with their assumption that if we just memorize the steps and follow the rules, we can perfect ourselves. Who wants perfect? Perfect is Botoxed and size six. God never intended for us all to look the same. Instead, this book will provide you with a context and a sense of community. Browse through these chapters gradually over time, or actually follow the steps for one weekend as described in "A Jumpstart Agenda" in the Afterword. You can enjoy the exercises with friends or go it alone. The weekend retreaters will affirm that it *is* possible to go away for a weekend and have a life-changing experience, and I urge each and every one of you to try to find that time. You can use the blank pages at the end to capture your growth or to keep a totally separate journal.

However you decide to use this book, I encourage you to purchase a journal and write as you read. Your reactions will form a conversation with my text and a springboard for your own original ideas. I saved all of my thoughts and exercises from that year alone, and I continually refer back to them for encouragement and inspiration. Although you may move in and out of the various sections as you see fit, do begin with the first chapter in order to understand your own need for change.

We are all sisters in this struggle to re-evaluate our routines and rules, and we need to encourage each other to take more risks. As T. S. Eliot once said, "Only those who risk going too far can possibly find out how far they can go."

So, if you have been yearning to find the real you, refresh your sagging spirit, be spontaneous, wild, and even free, enjoy the present, let go of control, recover a broken spirit, or retrieve the buried parts of you—this book is for you. This is your chance to live into your questions, change your routine, depart from the norm, question the status quo, and take back some of each day just for you. Life is, after all, simply a response.

There comes a time in every woman's life when she is called to account for herself. Is that time now for you? Sure, it will take some discipline, determination, trust, and time. But in the end, you will understand the words of Plato: "The unexamined life is the wasted life." So go ahead. Leap off that high dive, though the voices inside you say no. And then never look back. It is finally your turn.

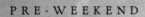

Understand Your Need for Change

Wake Up, Sister. It's Your Turn

"There is a fallow time for the spirit when the soil is barren because of sheer exhaustion."

HOWARD THURMAN

Recognize That You Are Lost

A full life requires cultivation. The minute we take our hands off the plow, fail to reseed, forget to fertilize, we've lost our crop. And yet most women I know have, in the service of some greater good, let their very lives wilt on the vine.

Having been taught the fine art of accommodation, most of us have developed a knack for selfless behavior. We've dulled our personal lives while propping up everyone else's, and we're no longer able even to imagine having any sort of adventure, romance, meaning, or purpose for ourselves. In short, we've gotten way off track and taken the wrong road to self-satisfaction, foolishly thinking that, after all of the do-

13

ing, giving, trying, and overworking, someone will offer us a reward. But Prince Charming was a bad joke, and all the fairy godmothers are dead. Instead of happy ever after, most of us end up with *the ache.* We wake up each day with an inner gnawing, a hunger for more, a craving for an overhaul, but we are too listless, tired, or depressed to do anything about it. We have spent the greater part of our lives pouring ourselves out like pitchers. No wonder we feel so empty. But we lack the necessary energy, a helpful roadmap, and any type of guidance and support. Well, it's time to change all of that.

The first step is to recognize that you are lost. In Ingmar Bergman's film *Face to Face,* Jenny, an accomplished yet empty woman, says: "We [women] act the part. We learn the lines. We know what people want us to say. In the end, it's not even deliberate, because we are so very conscientious about our behavior." It may seem almost impossible to get back behind the habit of performance to that raw-material person we once were. But it's not.

I was a suburban mother of two sons, a supportive wife to a busy man, a devoted daughter and daughter-in-law to four aging parents, and a reliable nurturer to multiple members of our extended family and friends. Chained to my agenda and telephone, I prided myself on being a multi-tasking wonder, fixing, along the way, my share of scraped knees, hurt feelings, and even some of my friends' failing marriages. Just call on me and I would happily run the school bazaar, handle the pledge drive for church, slice the oranges and pour the Gatorade for soccer and basketball games, all the while writing features for a local newspaper in order to earn some petty cash for extras. My calendar was so full that I took to taping extra paper onto the margins.

I would jump out of bed in the morning, throw on some clothes, make breakfast, pack the lunches, wave goodbye to everyone, clean up the kitchen, go for my walk, run errands, tackle my work assignments, return to the kitchen to prepare dinner and then do another round of cleanup, kiss everyone good night, and finally fall back into bed. For the most part, I performed so well that no one else even bothered to pitch in. If people did, I usually pushed their help away, confident that I had everything under control.

I was frenzied, but I felt important and full of my accomplishments. After all, didn't I produce the most beautiful dinner parties, holidays, and special family events? I was helping others, and both their progress and their smiles seemed like reward enough for me. My self-worth came from being the resident caretaker. It was as if I had been bred for the role.

In hindsight, I see that the training began back in puberty, when my body took on a life of its own. Once the hormones began to pop, the next forty years mapped themselves out for me. I was no stronger than my urge to mate, procreate, caretake—swept along all the way by the rush of giddy excitement, desire, and role-playing.

But eventually there was a downside to being this invisible sustainer, a hovering sense that I wasn't really as fulfilled as I thought. A pang of doubt would often sneak up on me unawares, when, for instance, my mother would help me serve dinner and repeat her age-old mantra: "Mothers always eat the chicken wings." It was a joke that went back to the Depression era, when a clever housewife was able to feed a family of six on one tiny roasted chicken. Yet, every time I heard my mother talk about taking the least desirable part of the bird, I felt sorry for her. After all, weren't mothers important? Didn't they need nutrition just as much as anyone else?

The doubting thoughts and questions became more frequent when our sons went to college. Blank spaces began to appear on the calendar, and I suddenly had too much time to spare. What should I do now? Distressingly, I hadn't the faintest idea. Enthralled with nurturing others, I had all but forgotten that I, too, had needs, desires, and goals. So I huddled with my girlfriends as we sipped too much wine and complained about our plight. We were all waking up to the stark reality that none of us had bothered to invest in our individual futures. What's more, my friend Cheryl concluded, "You don't get a gold watch for menopause!"

Searching for ways to assuage our ache, we began renting films about women at the crossroads, just to see how each protagonist found her way out of the quagmire. Ellen Burstyn ran away in *Alice Doesn't Live Here Anymore,* as did Shirley Valentine in the movie of the same name. Jill

Clayburgh escaped into a series of affairs in *An Unmarried Woman,* and poor Gena Rowlands simply went crazy in *A Woman Under the Influence.*

None of these stories really offered us a strong solution, so we each went our separate ways. Virginia applied to law school; Adelia got her real-estate license; Judy, a recent widow, took a lover, and together they started traveling the world; Helen "came out"; Julie embraced the joys of grand-mothering; and Cheryl ran off to her favorite island in Maine with her husband. I applauded my friends' actions, but their particular choices seemed to me to be more about finding something to do or a new relationship that would serve to distract them from their ache. I was craving some-thing else; I just couldn't seem to put my finger on it.

I suppose I was hoping for a sign or event—some kind of ritual to occur that would free me up for a new course and identity. There were rituals to be sure: my sons graduated from college and moved into their own homes; one got mar-ried; another engaged; my father died; my husband turned fifty. But all of these transitions revolved around others. Although I was intimately involved in and changed by these events, none of them put the focus on me. Once again I was producing special-occasion moments and then feeling let down after the intensity of the event dissolved.

Then, one Christmas, during a visit to the married chil-dren, I truly began to understand that I had to stop looking for help from others; any change in my life was mine to initiate. From the moment Robin and I arrived, I felt very much out of place. The children had a clear vision for the holiday, and though they had included touches from both of their families, most of the plans were unfamiliar to me. What was worse, all of my offers to help seemed to fall on deaf ears. I repeated to myself that children have to reject us in order to get on with their lives. But I wasn't prepared to handle the power shift, or my brand-new role as bit player. So I took to retreating to the bedroom to hide my awkwardness. I had learned long ago that the Chinese character for "conflict" is two women under the same roof, and regardless of my own discomfort, I was determined to have none of that.

If truth be told, I wanted my old role back. I wanted to continue to design and control the traditions—to make my grandmother's coffee cake, open our stockings, and then have brunch before presents, complete with eggs Benedict. But I had realized long ago that staying in the "I want" place was ego-driven—I want to still be important to my sons, I want holidays to be my way, I want traditions to stay as I have always dictated them. I needed to let go of my wants and start concentrating on "I am" in order to find a new life and the bliss I sought. It was time to take charge of becoming a new me, and the first step was to admit that I was lost.

Soon after Christmas, something strange happened that forced me to listen to my invitation further. I developed a sensation in my throat that gradually made it almost impossible to swallow. Esophageal cancer, I thought, or, at the very least, a bad case of acid reflux! I raced off to my internist in a panic. After several tests, she concluded that the presenting symptoms amounted to nothing. Rather than a prescription, she handed me a book she had just read, *You Can Heal Your Life,* by Louise Hay. In this little book, Hay explains how negative emotions and high anxiety frequently produce pain—the body's way of telling us to change our patterns and live differently. In my case, I had to admit that I simply couldn't swallow the way I was living anymore. So, despite my fears, the lonely work of finding a new self commenced.

The psychiatrist I had started seeing applauded my realizations. "Good for you for wanting to be your own heroine," she said. "It's difficult, isolating work. You've got to break with the patterns of your past—not an easily achievable endeavor for a compassionate woman such as yourself, but well worth the effort." Although she continued to raise my consciousness, she didn't tell me how to break from these stultifying patterns, how to appease my inner gnawing, or how to become my own heroine. I remained puzzled, at a loss as to how to proceed, and I continued to struggle with feelings of apathy, tedium, and stagnation.

A Leap of Faith

That's when fate intervened. My husband announced that he had found an exciting new job in a neighboring state and that we would be moving in two months. *We,* I found myself thinking—what gives with the assumed *we?* As I listened in disbelief, I found myself countering with a plan of my own—I would view his opportunity as a chance to do something for myself and take a short refuge in our Cape Cod cottage. The words were out of my mouth before they were formed, and I shocked us both. Previously after being loose-tongued, I would backslide and apologize for my desires and opinions. This time I didn't. Instinct told me to hold to the course.

But taking a leap is one thing—landing on your feet is quite another. It was an impulsive decision, to be sure, and I hadn't the faintest idea what I was in for until I arrived at the cottage, with no one there to greet me and no agenda for distraction.

Unlocking the door and walking into a place darkened by shades was anticlimactic in light of the commotion that had surrounded the announcement of my great escape. I quickly whipped the covers off the fading furniture and threw open the windows to clear the air of must. But nothing I did made me feel any less uncomfortable in this familiar place. So I hurriedly left my empty nest and raced off to the sea. Walking on the beach has always cured my jitters, and I eagerly anticipated the exhilaration of frothy waves and wild surf. Instead, I found a glassy sea with no visible energy or motion. On closer inspection, I noticed the familiar circle that indicates that it must be ebb tide—the time when the sea is neither coming in or going out, simply turning itself around. Perhaps, I concluded, the ebbing sea was meant as a sign for me to indulge in a sort of psychic slumber—that I, too, was to ebb—that being in neutral for a while might help soothe my aching soul.

For the next several days, I packed my duffel and went to the beach, plotting my arrival in time for the ebb. As I squatted in the dunes, gathering my knees up close to my chest and rocking to the rhythm of the water, I tried to look backward to discern a vision I must have had for my life before it ran amuck.

Although I could remember numerous events from long ago, the recent year was a total blur. It took hours to recall even the smallest detail, let alone the big moments. But, sticking with the exercise, I was finally able to recall my birthday, a trip out west, getting a writing assignment from a magazine, and being bedridden with a bad back. Once I had the year in focus, I spent a rainy day reflecting on each event: was it fun, exciting, difficult, unfortunate, sad, depressing? For the most part, my memory remained sketchy, and many of the experiences, in retrospect, just seemed downright exhausting.

I decided to put squares □ around all the exhausting moments, triangles △ around those that were exhilarating, hearts ♡ around any moments shared with my husband, and, finally, circles ○ around those activities that had been just for me. When I looked at the whole picture, I was more than startled. The page was, for the most part, all squares! What had started out as a little exercise turned into a major eye-opener. Surely I was living more for others than for myself, and I had given a lot more pleasure than I had received. I was exhausted, and what's more, it was my own fault. I had become an unwitting victim of my own obsessive planning, facilitating, and organizing!

The saddest example of all was our son's wedding. Because the bride's family lived so far away, I was left to organize the wedding on a tight budget. Although I thought I was having fun, I got so caught up in the minutiae of making sure it was perfect (of course) that I simply didn't remember a thing. Days later, I frantically ran off to have the film developed so I could see, and, I hoped, recall, all the pageantry and splendor that I had missed.

Give Your Life the Focus It Deserves

I'm slowly coming to the conclusion that it takes time and stillness to ask yourself during and after both major and minor events how you actually felt about them. "How did I feel about the surprise party I gave my husband?" Now, I don't mean: "How did the cake turn out? Did the guests have a good time? Did he like his presents? Was it better than the party he had thrown for me?" I mean: "How did I

feel? Did I enjoy doing it? Was the work exhausting or exhilarating? If I had it to do over again, would I even have
had the party? What did I want for myself going into this
party, and did I get it?" These are not questions we ask ourselves when we are busy sustaining others and playing the
roles.

I made a vow to myself after that rainy-day exercise to
go for more circles in next year's calendar, and I taped the
original, annotated one up on my fridge as a reminder. One
way to succeed, I concluded, was to begin to be more compassionate toward myself. There is not a woman I know
who doesn't get herself into trouble for being too compassionate; that one strength almost always turns out to be our
undoing. We extend our arms and hearts to take on the issues and problems of others until we can't hold any more—
least of all ourselves—and soon we find we are on the fast
road to empty.

My favorite author, Clarissa Pinkola Estes, calls this the
"be all things to all people" complex. She goes on to explain
in *Women Who Run With the Wolves:*

> *Women tend to take adequate time away to respond to
> crises of physical health—particularly of others, but neglect
> to make maintenance time for their own relationship to
> their souls. They tend to not understand soul as the central
> generator of their animation and energy. Many women*

drive their relationship to soul as if it were not a very important instrument. Like any instrument of value, it needs shelter, cleansing, oiling, and repair. Otherwise, like a car, the relationship sludges up, causes deceleration in a woman's daily life, causes her to use up enormous energy for the simplest tasks, and finally busts down, out on heart-break ridge, away from town and telephone. Then it is a long, long walk back home.

Her description of women is precisely why, after a lifetime of caregiving, we develop that subtle ache. It comes from missing our very selves. Deep inside we know that our own voices are going unheard and that we are the only audience they really need. We need to learn to turn our compassion around and embrace ourselves.

Hundreds of women have attended my Weekends by the Sea because they have finally decided not to leave themselves out of their lives. At our opening session, they share their reasons for coming. Some report huge events that almost toppled their lives—a husband being unfaithful; the death of a child, parent, or good friend; moving to a new city; being laid off from a job; getting divorced—but most speak simply of simmering feelings of discontent. They speak of a need to relax, replenish, and regenerate. They are searching for purpose, to dream again, to be present in their lives, to regain their confidence. Some just want to have fun, to escape tedious routine, to break out of their ruts. Whatever their reasons, once they are done, I walk them through the calendar exercise and their fates are sealed. Like mine, their calendars are covered with squares, and they can no longer deny that back behind their ache is a lost self. Whether they sensed it before or not, they now realize that in order to soothe their ache they need to find out who they are and who they want to be.

The Cluttered Calendar

What would your calendar look like? Do you have startling memories to jot down, or, like so many, would your mind simply draw a blank? It is important to remember that this exercise is to see just how much you do not recall (which is the same as not being present in your daily life), as well as how little you actually do for yourself.

Spend the next thirty minutes recalling last year. Start anywhere. Pick a month, and, without looking at your daybook, try to remember activities, events, and happenings that involved you, your career, and your family.

January _____

_____

_____

February _____

_____

_____

March _____

_____

_____

April _____

_____

_____

May _____

_____

_____

June _____

_____

_____

July _____

_____

_____

August _____

_____

_____

September _____

_____

_____

October _____

_____

_____

November _____

_____

_____

December _____

_____

_____

After listing as many events as you can recall, put a SQUARE around anything that was exhausting, a TRIANGLE around anything that was invigorating, a HEART around anything that you did with your partner or a family member, and a CIRCLE around anything that was just for you. Now answer the following questions:

· How do you feel about the past year?

_____

_____

_____

· What gave you pleasure? How and why?

_____

_____

_____

· What experiences were sources of pain? Why?

_____

_____

_____

- Were most of the events driven by you or by outside forces?

_____

_____

_____

Study your calendar. Know that your goal is to be part of a life that is not driven simply by the roles that you play and the things that you do, but also by the pleasure you experience.

Calendar Control

A recent weekender from Maryland best states the value of this exercise: "Doing the calendar exercise shocked me. I couldn't remember a thing from the previous year, yet I was always busy. Now I am more aware of how fast-paced life is, and I am becoming more conscious of what I am doing and how I am actually living. I have bought myself a package of self-stick stars. Every time I do something pleasurable or just for myself, I put a star on my calendar."

The value of the calendar exercise is not always immediately apparent. At one of my early weekends, a woman brought a resistant friend. She thought the weekend and my message were more about relationships, and as far as she was concerned, her marriage made her very happy. She cruised through the first part of the exercise, easily able to remember a full year's worth of events. But as she started to annotate her calendar, she slowed down, and I saw her posture collapse. I glanced over at her page and saw lots of squares and triangles, often around the same event. She had few hearts and fewer circles. When we were all finished, she was the first one to raise her hand. She practically shouted at the group:

I can't believe it. I feel ridiculous and almost like a traitor. I always thought that, because my husband and I were going to events together, the evenings had some value. But simply stopping and forcing myself to recall separately what I did and how I felt about it—was it invigorating or exhausting? was it for me?—made me see how little I do just because I want to. I have only two circles on my entire calendar—the weekend I spent with my sister planting her new garden, and the time I am spending here. I suddenly feel as if I'm not a part of my own life.

Regardless of how you feel as you begin the calendar exercise, it should become a catalyst for change. It acts as an awakening for most women who sense they are on empty but can't figure out why.

Because I have become so aware of time—knowing it,

collecting moments, living truly in the present—my calendar now (as compared with nine years ago) is well balanced with both exhausting and exhilarating moments, and it mostly includes events that are designed around my agenda. It's interesting to report that the women who have the most circles on their calendars talk about taking time away on an unusual trip, having a reunion with old female friends, challenging their bodies and souls by training for a marathon or having an outdoors adventure.

The point is that we must learn to accept and indulge ourselves. Little activities, such as having a massage during the holiday season, soaking in a bubble bath rather than finishing the dishes, and settling into bed with a pile of magazines in the middle of the afternoon, are good first steps. Eventually you will have to ask yourself some tough questions about goals, needs, damage done, and ways to have more joy. But for the moment, set aside one day next week just for you.

A full life does require cultivation, and most women's lives require some fallow time to restore our spirit, body, and mind. We must learn to experience our seasons (just as any fledgling plant must do), in order to bear fresh fruit. Whether you are thirty, forty, fifty, or sixty, the time is now. The most difficult step is always the first step—you don't have to take a grand step, but you must go ahead and open the door.

END OF CHAPTER SUMMARY

· Recognize that you are lost

· Acknowledge and explore your ache

· Confront your calendar

· Indulge yourself

But Versus *And*

This spring, just after I had returned from a book tour in which I crisscrossed the country in a matter of three weeks, a dear friend heard the exhaustion in my voice and sympathetically told me that what I really needed was to take one week off. I laughed and said, "Yes, but I have a book signing on Wednesday night." She tried to come up with some more suggestions for how to help me feel more relaxed, including just coming over and bringing me dinner and a bottle of wine. Nothing worked. All I could think about was the book signing and how it ruined my chance to take a week for myself. I was stuck in the *I want* and couldn't get myself into the *I am.* I was stuck on that damn *but.*

What would have happened if I had said to my friend, "Yes, I do need a week off. Thank you for caring. And I also have a book signing on Wednesday night"? First of all, the whole tone of the conversation would have changed and become more positive. My friend would not have felt dismissed, and I would have felt better simply for having been nice. Second, I would have seen that I have choices. Either I could find a way to see the book signing as part of my week off, or I could choose not to go. Yes, there is not enough time, and there never will be. It is up to me to find a way to manage the week.

How often do you find yourself asking a friend for advice and then, before her opinion is out of her mouth, you cut her off by saying, "But that isn't really possible because . . ." or "But I can't imagine doing that"? We think we want input and we are curious about someone else's idea, but our reaction reveals that we aren't really ready to move on or attempt a new approach to our problem.

I suppose it is human nature to want to make our own decisions and keep the power over our destiny in our own control. Yet, when we are stuck, we tend to look to others to help us out of our quandary. The trick to is let go enough to entertain new options. I have had many friends who have sought my advice as a sort of exercise—they enjoy polling others in order to gather pro and con opinions for a decision they will ultimately make for and by themselves. When I actually give my opinion, and they argue with my point of view or throw out the word *but,* I always know that after a time they will still be in the very same stuck spot.

I think one of the reasons *but* comes out so quickly—why focusing on what we want rather than where we are is so much easier—is that then we don't have to take action. We don't have to put ourselves forward. And how do we comfortably put ourselves forward when we have forgotten how to speak from our own needs and desires?

But is a stopping word. Inevitably when we use it we are attempting to slow down a process, keep things on hold, and, for the moment, not change the situation in which we find ourselves. When you change your *but* reaction to *and,* however, you are working toward opening up and including new possibilities. *And* is inclusive—it keeps things moving—it signals a person's willingness to add on ideas rather than stop action, to entertain change rather than stay stuck in the familiar. After my conversation with my friend, I experimented with my attitude, and I found that by changing how I spoke—and thought—I could be happier. In this instance, I chose to focus not on the fact that I couldn't take a whole week off and stay in bed, but, rather, on the fact that I had a full, rich life. That people were buying my books and cared to meet me. I turned the hurdle into a compliment and then looked at the rest of my calendar to see what other activities I could skip or rearrange.

The next time you seek advice, or are in a conversation, observe how many *buts* become part of the interaction. Make a mental note of when you used it and how doing so puts a hold on moving a thought, idea, or action forward. After a time, try not using *but* at all and see how it affects your day-to-day life. When we are stuck, choice is threatening because it implies change. When you accept your power over these choices, you will have begun the process of being more open and free.

STAR POWER

A quick and easy way to start making sure that you make time for yourself is to buy a package of self-stick stars and keep them beside your calendar. Every time that you manage to eke out a moment for yourself, place a star on that particular day. Before you know it, your calendar will glitter.

A friend of mine, who found it impossible to ever put herself first, thought up this simple idea. She loved seeing the shiny stars and consciously worked to get more and more of them up on her calendar. What's more, when her family asked why the calendar was covered in stars, she explained that they represented the times when Mommy was good to Mommy. This made sense to everyone, because it took away the threat implied in Mommy's using her time for herself rather than anyone else. After a time, when Mommy was off to have her nails done, or go for a long bike ride, or spend an afternoon with her friends, her family reminded her to give herself a star.

Star power is the easiest and fastest way to begin the process of self-care.

The Importance of Retreat

Selfhood Begins by
Walking Away

"Woman must come of age herself. She must find her
true center alone. She must become whole."

ANNE MORROW LINDBERGH

An Argument for Solitude

It has been nine years since my year by the sea. There have
been the comings and goings of family, watching both sons
become fathers, a husband in transition, a mother who, because of failing health, has moved nearby, and a career that
now has too many deadlines. Much has changed, but one
passion remains—my need to retreat and seek solitude each
day as a way to stay present, focused, and alive to my own
individual spirit.

In my talks with women throughout the country, I strive
to help them understand the merits of solitude and retreat.
For it is with solitude that we find the capacity to listen to

our own voices, take ownership of our lives and our ideas, and assuage *the ache.* But just how does a woman with extra paper taped to the edges of her calendar find solitude and stillness? There is only one way. She retreats. She dares to step away from the responsibilities, activities, and routines of her life in order to embrace the present moment and achieve an inner stillness.

We've talked about our busyness, our attentiveness to others, and *the ache* we all feel, but there is something else to be considered—our failure to give ourselves the proper time and space to honor the transitions that life doles out to us. Looking back at last year's calendar, how many of the events that you listed involved major transitions—that is, a time when something happened and changed your sense of self or of place? More important, after any one of those transitions, did you give yourself time alone to understand what had transpired and how you felt? Or did you just move quickly ahead, cell phone in one hand, car keys in the other? I've come to see that personal changes of any sort, big or small, can put our bodies and spirits in a state of shock. Left unprocessed, this shock sets down roots that wrap themselves around our souls and inevitably leave us with *the ache.*

In my case, a confluence of events crowded my spirit and sent me packing to Cape Cod. My husband's move was certainly the catalyst, but so was the fact that my father died suddenly, our two boys left home, a best friend moved to Maine, and a collaborator with whom I had worked on many children's books chose to end the partnership. The pattern of my life had changed irrevocably. Nothing was the same. I was living on foreign soil, and I instinctively knew that only if I processed the grief that always accompanies change could I regain my equilibrium. The more change we have in our lives, the more transitions and pain with which we have to contend. The little and big endings we endure all leave wounds that must be healed, and who can ever tell how long this will take?

When my husband and I lived in East Africa, it was fascinating to see our African friends leave town when someone close to them died. We knew better than to ask when they would return. They would simply be away until the grief they felt had been processed and the mourning concluded. Shakespeare, too, knew the logic of this when he said: "He who lacks time to mourn, lacks time to mend." And yet our culture tells us to cut our losses—say goodbye to the old and get on with the new as quickly as possible— no use crying over spilt milk—what's done is done. How wonderfully efficient and productive all this sounds!

Recently I was asked to speak at a conference for oncology nurses. It occurred to me that if anyone knew about transition it was this group. I thought of what their days must be like as they care for cancer patients—some going into remission, others suffering recurrences, many dying. Surely they perform holy work. I suggested to these special women that, instead of moving expeditiously from one crisis to another, every time they experienced a passage they should take themselves off to a quiet space, out into the light of the day or the dark of the night. There, apart from their duties and skills, they should stand for a minute or two, breathe, and think about what had just occurred, the role they played in the event, and how it made them feel. I was heartened after my speech when several nurses came up to me with a new plan: they were going to meet in the nurses' lounge at the beginning of their shift, stand in a circle, hold hands, and breathe energy into each other as a way to prepare for the tumult of the day.

When I shared this story with a friend, she sat up and said: "Right. The pause—that's what we forget. How can we cope with anything if we don't take at least a moment to pause?"

Retreat is a form of pause—it is a time apart in solitude, a precious space in which we can see our world in a different light—acknowledge the grief, celebrate the gifts, and honor our own unique spirit without worrying about how others see us or what jobs still have to be done. For me, retreat is a time to endure suspense; find, not seek; relish what comes by chance; repair body and soul; wait patiently; and live into the questions. It is a time to get acquainted with silence—that friend we've kept at a distance; a time to be open to the spaciousness of a day; a time to live on the other side, in another world, where spirit, deep thought, and a new kind of wonder can flourish. Above all, retreat is a time to honor all that we have experienced and the way it affects our hearts.

Webster's dictionary defines "retreat" as the "act or process of withdrawal ... a receding from a position" to a place that affords peace, privacy, and security. But I prefer Jennifer Louden's assertion that retreat is "an act of self-nurturing, a radical leap into the hallowed halls of selfhood."

Become a Scholar of Self and Soul

The women who travel to the shores of Cape Cod to retreat with me for a weekend come because their instincts told them to wake up, push through the blur of busyness, and admit, as Robert Frost says, that "they are lost enough to find themselves." In short, they are ready to rid themselves of a life that was laid out for them, and ready to embrace a life of their own planning and execution. They are no longer satisfied with responding to everyone else's needs while neglecting their own. They are heroines who have accepted that, in order to find themselves, in order to reconnect with their own buried dreams and desires, they must first step away from the clutter and chatter of everyday life and seek solitude.

On Friday, when I first greet these women, I take pains

to praise them for simply getting away. Many have left behind people who will label them selfish; others have left young children with an assortment of sitters or confused husbands. They have walked away from a car that needs brakes, a stack of bills to be paid, an empty refrigerator, a garden full of weeds. Still, they arrive with determination and great anticipation. It is as if they have enrolled in a graduate course designed just for them. They are here to become scholars of self and soul—to study their strengths and weaknesses, mistakes and triumphs. Even so, walking away from familiar routines and relationships, for any amount of time, takes courage and a fierce determination. As one retreater wrote to me:

> *Many changes in my life led me to crave the comfortable, the familiar, the safe. I believed that I could find security and sanity only in places, people, and routines that left no opening for the unknown. What I didn't see was that this determination to stick with the familiar was draining my spirit of life. Gradually, I began to think that maybe I needed more than the predictable, and that the way to breathe new life into my neglected soul might be to momentarily cast off my roles and create the space to reconnect with myself. Around that time, I read* A Year By the Sea *and decided to go on one of the weekend retreats. That first retreat was very frightening to me. I was so afraid of stepping outside of my routines, because they made me feel safe.*

I had an especially hard time looking at all the transitions
I had experienced, because, I realized, I was afraid to start
grieving. But a whispered voice inside cried, "Save me"—
and I listened.

There is always a risk when you do something new and buck the system, but in order to thrive, we must take the time to cultivate our depths and go to that inner place where so many resources have been buried. For fresh meaning to surface, we must dare to journey along the unpredictable, unfinished edges of our lives and, for a moment at least, to be alone.

Are you ready to explore all that is unfinished in your life and soul? A good way to start is to look at how your life has brought you to this searching place by evaluating the effect transitions have had on your psyche. By answering the following questions, you will start to appreciate the underlying reasons driving you to seek more time for yourself.

- **Have you lost a relationship in the past year or two?** *Has a spouse died, a friend moved away, a child left home? Have you been alienated from someone close? Has a pet died or a child gotten married?*

- **Has your home scene changed?** *Has a spouse retired or been laid off and is he now home all the time? Was someone ill that needed your care? Did you move, remodel, or get remarried?*

- **Have you experienced personal change?** *An illness, success or failure, a diet or a new exercise regime, a sleep disturbance, or financial problems?* *

Any of these changes upsets the equilibrium of your existence. Give yourself one point for each transition. A score of four or more, coupled with a calendar full of squares, should be proof enough that it is time to retreat.

When you are ready to plan your first retreat, you must be willing to set aside a significant block of time to wander, to empty yourself of the past, and to disconnect from your present worries and agendas. This will take careful planning, but the rewards will last you a lifetime.

One Woman's Retreat

A few months back, Denise, a woman who wanted a longer retreat than just a Weekend by the Sea, came to stay in my little guesthouse. Up until then, she had always lived behind a mask—never sure how to measure up to the culture's standards for women, a casualty of her own harsh judgment and insecurity. Her weekend retreat gave her a taste of what it was like to live without the mask and to revel in just being herself. But when she returned home, she knew she had

---

*William Bridges, *Transitions: Making Sense of Life's Changes*.

only touched the tip of the iceberg. Perhaps, coming from the heartland, she had an innate knowledge that retreating for a time might offer the same benefits as leaving a parcel of farmland unworked so that the soil can be revitalized. She sensed a need for a natural restructuring of her life—a chance to let her body and mind have their own way for a change.

She picked her time carefully, knowing that her husband would be on a business trip for half of her six-week stay and that she would have finally finished the course work toward a master's degree in social work. This planning allowed her to minimize any competing claims on her time and attention, and to feel more comfortable about leaving.

She arrived with books, a camera, some needlepoint, and exercise equipment. At first, she felt as if she were on vacation, and as a result had a difficult time withstanding the pangs of guilt she felt for her "indulgence." My guest had many personal hurdles to overcome as she attempted to discard a surplus of anxiety and rage, but one of her most visible struggles was with the empty, activity-less time she spent alone.

"Let yourself happen," I told her as she pondered how to be still. "Find a new forest or beach to explore, somewhere without familiar landmarks or people to ask for direction." Soon I would see her venturing off for a daily walk on the beach, followed by time alone in her cabin, and then a jaunt on a bicycle or in her car for places unknown. She was learning the art of lingering as she discovered her own haunts. She was becoming a living example of Joan Erikson's logic: "We do not receive wisdom—we discover it for ourselves after a journey through the wilderness."

Denise pushed on, testing her grit while hiking in the sands of the province lands, venturing out on treacherous jetties, or taking cover during several nor'easters with only candles for light and no apparent rescue. As she became more comfortable with the woods and shore, a new light could be seen through the cracks and chinks of her armor. Her body relaxed, the lines on her face disappeared, she seemed to walk with more determination and presence, and her porch became cluttered with numerous gifts from the sea—shells, rocks, buoys, and driftwood.

Another important step was her commitment to changing the rhythm of her day and dropping old habits. "I needed to break with the past, and one way I did that was to go on a technological fast," she said. "For my entire retreat, I avoided all contact with television, radio, cell phone, or e-mail. I kept myself focused on what I was doing and how I was feeling." I'm sure this radical change was difficult—one or two times, though no more, I caught her listening to the strains of music coming from my open windows. But by doing so she gained a detachment from the real world that rendered her more serene than she had ever felt before. Meals became more ceremonial than functional. Eating had come to be something she did on the run, infrequently sitting down to dine with her husband, and often in front of the news. Now she set the table for one, lit several candles, and dined on fresh fish and organic vegetables bought from a local farmer.

As she emptied her mind and spirit, as she pushed her body, affirmations appeared everywhere. On one of her forays out to the tip of a jetty, she encountered a fisherman who stared down at her and exclaimed, "Well, here's one brave woman." Another day she stumbled upon a beached dory with the words HOPE painted on its bow, and, sitting on its seat, she sensed then and there that she was indeed filling up with newfound hope.

While she was in residence, another past retreater, Linda, stopped by. The three of us shared a sandwich at the beach one day, and compared notes on why we had all needed to take the drastic step of walking away in order to turn our lives around.

"I had the perception that, because I was changing and life around me was changing—you know, like the kids moving out, a husband retiring, menopause, even a debilitating illness—" Linda confided, "the me inside would automatically change. But that proved false," she said, chuckling at her own naïveté. "After my first Weekend by the Sea, I returned home thinking that I felt different and had changed enough. But then I came to see that it would take many more such weekends to truly shed the roles and empty out the past. We women can never really declare that we have retired, can we?" she asked, looking puzzled. "It seems our roles are so firmly established that they don't shift much—that is, until we see the work that needs to be done to evacuate one person and haul in another! I could never do that work in the midst of my life. I needed to retreat and be by myself."

"How spacious life becomes when on retreat," I marveled, and we all shook our heads in unison. "When we get rid of the rules and shoulds, there really is so much room. Not to mention the fun of dressing down or not dressing at all!"

"But it did take several retreats before I could truly do my own thing," Linda continued. "A future can't be revealed to anyone in one full swoop. Each time I came, I stayed a little longer, shedding one role or another, I suppose, until, eventually, I felt unencumbered and available to me! It's no more complicated than being out of the ordinary; it has to do with being someplace mentally where I can receive the direction of my own spirit."

Courting Retreat—Starting Small

It is valuable to practice retreating in increments by carving out ritualized spaces of solitude and stillness. You don't need a full weekend to experience the benefits of retreating. Start small—begin to find mini-moments in your day when you can be still and alone. Although it appears in my book,

A Year by the Sea, as if I just took off as a knee-jerk reaction, the truth is that I had been harboring such thoughts since my boys were in high school. For a long time, before I had the gumption to "run away," I would indulge in mini-retreats. One of my original hiding places was the local Catholic church—the only place in the community that kept its doors unlocked. I would frequent its dark sanctuary, sit quietly in the back pew, and process my confusion and pain. As Thomas Merton once said: "There must be a time of day when we, who make plans, forget our plans and act as if we had no plans at all. There must be a time of day when we who have to speak fall very silent."

Gradually, I allowed for more time away—traveling out of town and into nature, "to a place that demands being open to the flow of life," as Lawrence Kushner said, "a place that demands being honest with yourself without regard to the cost of personal anxiety." For me, that place was a state park along the Hudson River. At first I would go to hike on its varied paths and drink in the colors of fall. When snow-fall came, I took my cross-country skis and retreated deeper into the forests, where only little animal creatures seemed to go. In the spring, I took picnic lunches and sat amidst the budding trees and fresh greenery. These hours away, in si-lence, graced me with peace of mind, and I found myself wanting to extend my stays. It quickly became apparent that I had developed a relationship with solitude—the stillness and silence I experienced when I spent hours alone were more valuable than visits to psychiatrists or workshops or lectures on selfhood.

"But," you say, "I have no time!" Nonsense, there is always time. To be precise, there are 86,400 seconds in every day, each second waiting to be used, wanting to be lived. Perhaps because we can't see or touch time, we don't understand the gift that is ours—that if we don't use our daily allotment as best we can we end up, once again, with *the ache*. We all have enough time; we simply misuse it.

One of the main reasons I ran away to the Cape was that my life was not my own, which boiled down to the fact that I was not in control of my time—that seconds, minutes, hours, and whole afternoons were spent in the service of others. It was as if I was doing time but not being in it. Perhaps that is why, in order to slow down, be in the moment, trust time, and make it mine, I took to watching my hourglass—turning it over and over again to watch the sand flow. As grain after grain would slip through the tiny opening, I gradually became more conscious of my day, and in so doing, I began to honor even the milliseconds—most especially when I realized that the sand never flows upward, that a second spent is a second gone.

Do you have time to go to the hairdresser's? To talk with a friend on the phone? To fold your laundry? Then you have time to spend in silence and stillness with yourself. I am not suggesting that any of the other activities that fill your day are no longer worth your time. I certainly get my hair cut every six weeks and enjoy regular talks with family and friends. But there is always an activity that can be skipped now and then, or shortened, or perhaps even abandoned altogether. In my house, for instance, folded laundry rarely makes it into any drawer. Anyone who has the will to change can carve out mini-moments for retreat.

- **Where could you go for an hour?** *Try to list at least ten possible places. There doesn't have to be anything dramatic about the places. They simply need to afford you the chance for one hour of uninterrupted solitude. Could you go to a park, library, bathroom, car, garden, hammock, the zoo, a museum, hiking, biking, Barnes & Noble, fishing, kayaking, or a room of your own?*

- **Where could you go for an overnight or a weekend?** *This may be more difficult, but try to come up with five places. Remember, at this point, to keep your focus on the place, not the myriad of logistics you would need to take care of before actually getting there. Too often we paralyze ourselves worrying about the hurdles before we even allow ourselves to envision the possibility of escape. But I've found that if I can just start imagining a destination, I can find ways to get there. Making a plan gives you power, and feeling power gives you hope.*

- **Where could you go for longer?** *Fantasize.*

- **Would you need help in order to escape? Where could you get that help?** *Again, don't rule out any possibility. Do you have relatives living nearby? Neighbors with whom you could offer a trade? Can you arrange a combination of playdates and sitters? If work is the issue, what exactly is your vacation and sick-leave policy? What other plans did you have for the year? How much do you want to do them? Were you sick a lot last year? Is your boss approachable for extra time?*

Return to these lists again and again as you incorporate retreat into your life. Most of my weekend women, once back home, have become very creative about finding ways to make retreat a part of their daily and weekly life. But they have also learned to do it in increments, picking their time carefully, and taking the current when it serves.

Once you have grown comfortable with regularly stepping away, start using your retreats to focus on your sense of self. Leave your house and go to one of the places you listed above. Take nothing with you except a journal and a pen. Let yourself be led to a spot—a place that calls to you—near a brook with running water, under a willow tree, upon a rock that seems made for sitting, a fallen log. React to your peace, the secret spot, the special moment, noticing all that is offered you.

- What do you hear, smell, or see?

Open your journal and record what comes to mind—single words, whole thoughts, memories of times past. As questions arise, write them down as well, but be careful not to search for answers; rather, live into the questions. Let this be a time of discovery and receiving. Stay in the ebb, that in-between place where everything is fluid. If you find yourself thinking about life beyond this place, cancel the thought and focus on an object around you. *Be still and listen* is a good mantra. Repeat that phrase or one of your choosing. You will see that in fifteen minutes or so you will be in a place of peace. Once you are there, you might think on some thoughts.

- What am I yearning for?
- What am I seeking?
- What must I eliminate from my everyday life?
- What do I need more of?

Let your thoughts flow through without censoring or second-guessing them. Let your mind wander as freely as your feet did. You might just be surprised at some of the answers you get.

Before leaving any retreat, celebrate your accomplishment of finding and maintaining peace with a ritual of praise, thanksgiving, and small petitions for continued grace and gentle changes. Inscribe in your journal praise for what you did to get here and what you have found, thanksgiving for what you possess, and petition for the strength to continue to take your life seriously. You are finally gifting yourself.

The Extended Retreat

Every weekend I host, one woman or another asks if I am advocating that we all run away from our marriages, families, and homes for a year. Linda, Denise, and I were able to retreat into solitude for extended periods of time. As a result, we were able to step away fully from the demands of our daily lives, and, while living in a new place, to give over to the whispered directions and requests of our hearts. I believe that any woman truly intent on rediscovering herself must find a way to take an extended retreat. But it does not have to be for a year or even six weeks. A weekend is plenty of time for most seeking women.

For the big escape, pick your time or take advantage of an unexpected turn of events. Obviously, when the kids are sick, you are running a benefit, it's holiday time, or your husband is closing on a big deal—these are not good times to run away. Taking leave of the family takes planning.

A good way to begin is to find a cabin or an isolated spot and go with a few friends. Schedule alone time during the weekend, and use your together time to compare notes on what each of you discovers. Keep the focus on *you* and the goal on time out, but use each other for support and, of course, the joy that comes from companionship.

There really are no more excuses. We dull our own lives by the way in which we conceive of them. It is time to change your mind-set. Add the flair and passion that you have been craving. For, as the writer Tove Ditlevsen said, "There is a young girl in me who refuses to die."

END OF CHAPTER SUMMARY

- Identify recent transitions
- Find your place
- Retreat

Knowing Your Sense of Place

I come from a family that was born on wheels. My father worked for a major oil company that transferred us a good seventeen times, and for most of my childhood and young adulthood, I felt placeless. The one place where I felt anchored was Cape Cod—a little peninsula that sticks out into the middle of the Atlantic Ocean to which we traveled every summer. Each year it felt as though we were going on a pilgrimage. My brother and I would peer out the car windows on the long drive, waiting and watching for familiar landmarks. First we would notice sandy soil at the edges of the highway; then the occasional salt marsh, cranberry bog, or inlet; and, finally, we would cross over the tall Sagamore Bridge and look down at the tiny white sails drifting on the Canal. Once we actually pulled into the driveway of whatever cottage we happened to be renting, we would make a beeline for the beach, promising, with our fingers double-crossed, not to get wet.

Wallace Stegner explained in his now famous essay "A Sense of Place," "No place is a place until things have happened in it and are remembered in history"—most importantly, personal history. When visiting such a place, you experience a kind of knowing that doesn't involve maps or road signs. In the case of Cape Cod, it is all about the smell of pine, salt air, and chowder on the two-burner stove, the feel of sand in my shoes, and the rustle of bayberry bushes. Any one of these sensations transports me back in time and wraps me in contentment. It was no accident that I sought refuge on Cape Cod.

So the question becomes: Where is your place? What beckons you? Where is it you find yourself returning again and again, either in fact or in memory? Is it some distant shore or lakefront where you went as a child, or the open space of the desert, dotted with cactus and well-worn red clay paths? Perhaps you are drawn to mountains that beckon you to climb just a little bit higher, or deep, lush forests that tempt you with secrecy and cover. Whatever the place or space, when you are there you are assured of important intangibles—a feeling of safety and warmth, the desire to wander and explore with your body and also your soul. Knowing your sense of place and getting there is the first step toward a serious retreat.

THINGS I WALKED AWAY FROM

The weekend women leave much behind when they decide to travel to Cape Cod. Over the course of the weekend, as they come to understand the value of retreat, they also realize that walking away is a state of mind as much as a physical act and that sometimes you can gain a sense of retreat and personal strength by walking away from even the littlest things. Here, in their own words, are some of the things that they have walked away from.

A husband

The office holiday party and the need to send out Christmas cards every year

The television

Parents

Cooking dinner—I taught my son the number for pizza delivery

An Internet lover

The weeds in my garden and a flat of new impatiens

A job

Sunday-afternoon football

A burdensome or toxic conversation

Someone else's need for me to get up from the couch

An argument

A ringing telephone

Chairing the PTA

The laundry

A dentist appointment

Weeknight sex

Hosting the annual neighborhood Memorial Day cocktail party

High heels and hose

Dirty dishes

Painted nails

Therapy

Alcohol

....

Retrieve Your Raw
Material Self

Put Yourself Back Together, Piece by Piece

"When you cannot go further, it is time to go back and wrest out of the past, something shining."

DAVID SCHUBERT

Sturdy Roots

So much goes into planning and preparing for a journey. No matter where I am going or for how long, I need to harness all of my drive and focus just to pack my bags, organize the piles I am leaving behind, and actually get out of the house. Then the journey itself begins, and I realize that I have spent so much energy in getting going that I have no idea how to proceed. This was certainly the case when I came to Cape Cod nine years ago: I had neither a plan nor a precedent to follow, and very little energy. For a while I relied on the habits I had acquired as a vacationer, but they didn't help me understand the change I had initiated or figure out what to do next. They provided me with activity, but no new answers to the nagging questions: Who was I now that I had run away? How was I supposed to reconstruct my life? What material did I have to work with?

One day, as I idly straightened up the house and tried to figure out what to do with the afternoon, my eyes settled on a bookcase at the end of the living room. The shelves were bulging with photograph albums and memorabilia. The bindings were well worn, and most of the books had been hastily shoved back into a space. My boys used to love rummaging through those shelves on rainy summer days, but it had been years since I spent any time with them.

On instinct, I pulled down a particularly familiar-looking album. It was one that my brother and I had made for our parents' twenty-fifth wedding anniversary. In it we had carefully arranged pictures of what we viewed as the big events of their lives: their courtship and wedding day, our births, Christmases and birthday celebrations, our school plays, and our summer vacations. There we were frolicking naked in the South Carolina surf; or looking as angelic as cherubs in the church pageant; or standing proudly beside the giant, lopsided snowman we had arduously constructed. There are summer pictures in which I am running gleefully through a cold sprinkler, dangling precariously from a jungle gym, and learning to play hopscotch on the sidewalk in front of the house. In all of the pictures, I have an unabashed grin, wonder-filled eyes, and a clear love of silly behavior.

But halfway through the album, I seemed to have changed. The once-perky little girl had turned chubby and sedentary. Her eyes didn't twinkle defiantly anymore, and she appeared awkward, rigid, and downright distant. I began removing close-ups and pictures of me alone. I laid them out across the living-room floor in some semblance of chronological order, hoping to make sense of myself. As I studied my body language, I noticed something else as well—how often the background changed. At the very end of the album, my mother had added a two-page spread full of pictures of each of the houses we had lived in over the years, and I remembered the pain I felt each time we were made to move. I was only six or seven the first time, and the terrifying thought of saying goodbye to everything I had ever known and moving to the faraway hills of Pennsylvania made me sob uncontrollably.

With each subsequent move, I grew increasingly skilled at stuffing my feelings. The pictures revealed just how adept I also became at looking around and sizing up the dominant tone, attitude, or style of my new classmates and neighborhood friends. I saw that, as much as the backgrounds changed, so did my clothes and hairstyle. I remembered that the early weeks in any new location were spent shaping myself to fit in so that I could feel as if I belonged, claim a group of friends, and identify with the new town. But not only did the repeated dislocation dampen my spirits, my need to conform pushed my individual voice underground. I became an echo of whatever tune played the loudest in my new milieu. I aimed to please, and I avoided any conflict or hint of originality. I was living proof of the truth behind the writer Wendell Berry's claim, "If you don't know where you are, then you don't know who you are." Some things never change, I thought with wry despair. Here I am, fifty years old, I've voluntarily uprooted myself once more, and I feel as lost and confused as ever.

I continued to sift through the pictures, now permanently spread out on the kitchen table. Studying my early life in this way was addictive, and, like an archeologist who had finally come across a long-lost kingdom, I was hell-bent on finding every last shard with which to piece together my story. I reached for the dusty older albums, the ones whose bindings had long ago fallen apart and been repaired with tape. Inside, beneath the old pictures, my mother had dutifully inscribed each person's name with either a birth date or the date he or she had come into this country. So many of my kin were immigrants—great-uncles, aunts, and a grandfather were all photographed arriving at Ellis Island from Switzerland, Germany, and Scotland, sitting on benches with just one suitcase apiece, and probably very little cash or command of the English language. But all of them looked hopeful, and their body language spoke of determination, independence, and stubbornness. Instead of embracing the impulses of my distant relatives, I seemed to have simply lost my grit. How does someone who was raised from such courageous stock get stopped or derailed?

Looking back at my childhood reminded me that who I had become and how I felt were part of a reaction to the circumstances of my life. Just as so many of us do—men as well as women—I had let those circumstances get the best of my individuality. This had been particularly easy for me because, each time we relocated, my family became more alone. There were pictures of my brother, my parents, and me with various friends, but only ever a photo or two of any one face. Our extended family appeared once or twice a year, in holiday shots or for an occasional visit, and the albums I scoured lacked any continuity of friendly, familiar faces. It was easy to see that my connection to my extended family had been sorely diluted, but what I found next was a crucial lesson in perspective and the sturdiness of our roots.

The Black Sheep Leads the Flock

Stuffed into a bulging envelope, I came across a bunch of pictures of my dear Aunt Elsie, my mother's sister, and I sat there staring at them with a broad smile on my face. She was wild and outrageous. We all wanted to sit next to Aunt Elsie and be the special beneficiary of her shared stories. And yet I hardly smiled the time my uncle compared me to her. "She was bold, bossy, and outrageous, just like you," he had said. I remember turning red and wishing that I had been compared to one of the kinder, gentler aunts. Aunt Elsie was fun, but she was also the black sheep of the family and everything a woman shouldn't be—she'd had a child out of wedlock, given it up for adoption, and was "kept" by the lawyer for whom she was a secretary.

At the time of my uncle's comment, I was still caught up in being a nice girl who played by the rules and was accepted, but now I see what a compliment he had given me. At this point in my life, I would far prefer to be compared to a colorful, lively, unconventional relative than to one of the meek and mild ones. After all, Aunt Elsie, with all her drama, turned out to be unsinkable—a veritable liberated woman a half-century before Betty Friedan. What's more, she lived her life with abandon: educating herself and traveling the world with her lover. My favorite picture of her was taken aboard the *Mauritania* as they were departing for Europe: waving from the promenade deck, champagne glasses in their hands, streamers dangling; she is draped in furs and jewelry. As always, Aunt Elsie is grinning, and her eyes twinkle.

I had been gazing at that picture for a long time when, suddenly, I noticed that Aunt Elsie and I had the same broad forehead. In fact, we shared more than a forehead—we had the same jowls, the same bone structure, and the same smile. I got up and checked my face in the mirror. Yes, indeed, for all intents and purposes, that could have been me standing on that ship! And if I shared her bone structure and smile, if my spirit had once reminded my uncle of hers, maybe I wasn't as lost or alone as I thought.

That one old picture helped me to see that, no matter how often I moved or how many times I changed my hairstyle or bought new clothes, I had sturdy roots. As my memories of Aunt Elsie took on a different tone, memories of other female relatives rushed forward. There was quiet, stubborn Grandma Lee who always had her purse on her arm, ready for any adventure; glamorous Aunt Vallie who sewed her own high-fashion dresses out of leftover bed linens; brave Aunt Minnie who remained on the farm in Minnesota to raise her four kids after her husband died; incorrigible Grandma Jo, who refused to stop smoking despite her doctor's appeals. The women in my family were bold, fun, feisty, incorrigible, brave, glamorous, independent, and willful, and it was high time I owned my genes. So I raised my coffee cup to Aunt Elsie and all of my other female relatives who had not just survived but actually thrived in the living of their lives, despite what anyone said or thought of them, and I came up with a plan.

Make a New Creation Out of the Old Self

I would embrace the grab bag of experiences I had inherited from my female relatives, as much to honor them as to save myself. Clarissa Pinkola Estes advised as much when she wrote: "The old values, even if one has to dig for them and relearn them, support the soul and the psyche. The old ways are a form of nutrition that never spoils and actually increases the more one uses them. In any case, not to use the legacy and soulful values severs a woman from her very important matrilineal lines."

As a first step, I wrote down the attributes I admired most in my female relatives and hung them over the kitchen sink, to remind me both to loosen up and to stretch myself a bit. If I chose *carefree,* I either stayed in bed all day with a pile of magazines or canceled any previous plans and went hiking or kayaking alone; if I chose *wild,* I ran naked into the waves without regard for the weather. As my year by the sea went on, I needed to be *independent* in order to survive financially. I quickly developed the *will* to find a job and the *guts* not to play it safe, but work until my fingers were cracked and my muscles ached at a fish market. Further, it was *feisty* to try my hand at clamming and *brave* to hire a boat and go camping alone at North Beach.

Little by little, I developed a "why not" response to every idea or inclination that popped into my head, and I felt my ancestors cheering me on from the grave. If I had an invitation, I wouldn't sit and deliberate, I acted with spontaneity and conviction. I said yes more and more, knowing that I had been born to do so. Things were changing, and only for the better. I had been wishing for a sense of passionate potential and finally was beginning to own some—all because I was able to see the deep reserve of strength I had at my disposal.

Relative Ability

When I first planned my Weekend by the Sea Retreats, there was no question but that a similar exercise should be part of the program, and the sooner it happened in the weekend, the better. So now I ask all the women to arrive with pictures and stories of a female relative they admire, and on the very first evening we talk about "relative ability."

Many women come without a picture, claiming that they were too intimidated by the assignment and drew a blank when they tried to think about one ancestor they would aspire to be. Others immediately raise their hands, eager to laud assorted mothers and grandmothers. More often than not, these admired relatives turn out to be magnificent caretakers—women who persevered in the face of financial hardship, absent husbands, or severe illness.

I listen hard, trying to find some adjective to put up on the easel. I want the women to see all that they have to unearth from their gene pools, but I also want them to escape the syndrome of self-sacrifice. As the evening wears on, eventually a story emerges that sets the discussion on the course I intended. At a recent weekend, Mary Beth from

Georgia thought she was going to espouse the greatness of her self-sacrificing grandmother. But as she stared at the framed picture sitting on her lap, she realized that, even though her grandmother was the only adult who truly seemed to care about her, this same woman turned out to be bitter, resentful, and unfulfilled.

Mary Beth's eyes filled up as she remembered the way her grandmother banged around the kitchen preparing dinner, never sharing the work or inviting others in, never even listening to music. Once the meal was prepared, she served it up with militaristic precision and ate in silence. There was no joy. On her deathbed, she confessed to Mary Beth that she had done it all wrong. "Take more for yourself, honey," her grandmother said. "That's the least you can do for me." The more she thought about it, Mary Beth concluded, the real heroine in her life was probably her mother. The entire family, Mary Beth included, had resented her mother when she walked out and left her father, even though everyone knew that she was in fact removing herself from an abusive relationship. She waited until the children had moved out of the house and then ran off to Florida. Luckily, Mary Beth happened to have a picture of her mother with her. When she dug it out of her knapsack, there were actual gasps.

"That's your mother?!" one of the women exclaimed.

"Not possible," said another. "How old is she?"

Everyone was amazed at the picture of a woman dressed in a shocking-pink sundress, strolling down a boardwalk, her body language free and content, her smile natural. No one could believe that she was in her seventies.

"I think it is her energy that I have come here to recapture," Mary Beth mused. "My mother was daring, rebellious, a little crazy, certainly a rule-breaker, and kind to herself. Having any one of those attributes would help turn me around." I quickly put those words on the easel.

"I had an Aunt Margie," said another. "She had a cackling laugh and wouldn't be browbeaten into anything. She always dressed in gypsy skirts or bohemian outfits from Putamayo. She was divorced twice, and happy to live alone in a small apartment decorated with wall hangings she brought back from India, and fruit-crate tables covered in silk. She was one of the first vegetarians I ever knew, and I could always count on a hot curry dinner when I went to visit."

Up on the easel go more wonderful adjectives.

"My Grandma Geri was amazing as well," said Cindi. "She became a radical in the 1960s, and when she was sixty-four, she took off on a Greyhound bus bound for Berkeley. She lived in a furnished one-room apartment, waitressed to make ends meet, and carried placards to protest the Vietnam War. Everyone was shocked, not least of all my grandpa. She returned a year later and resumed living with him, but not like before. He was a control freak, but now her timetable was to her liking. She ran the local Democratic Party and rented a bus to take all of her new friends to the

March on Washington." We added the words *independent,*
liberal, determined, radical, and *wild* to the easel.

One woman talked about her Aunt Mamie, an artist,
who painted only nudes, from live models, and to make this
possible turned her dining room into a makeshift studio.
Adelia's aunt traveled the world after she became a colonel
in the Army. "We called her simply 'the Colonel'—she was
one of the first women with rank. She fought in several
wars and would never rely on a man to get her out of a jam."
Charlotte reported having not one but two grandmothers
who got divorced (unheard of sixty years ago). One was an
organist in the church and ran off with someone in the
choir.

No matter how long it takes to get us started, the tenor
invariably changes over the course of the evening. The discussion marks the beginning of a breaking of the cycle as the
women begin to grasp their choices. Even those women
who still cannot hold up a relative of their own, feel em-
powered because any attribute on the easel is up for grabs.
Once shared, the stories of one woman's aunt or grandmother are available for anyone in the group to claim;
there's plenty of relative ability to go around.

Most of the women go to bed believing that they have
begun not only an incredible journey, but one that can actually work. Restrictions on what is possible have eased, and
horizons have broadened. Their task before the morning is

to study the variety of characteristics recorded on the easel and pick one or more to embrace for their future. I call these *intentions*—the very words act as an incentive for new behavior. When they leave on Sunday, each woman will take home a rock on which I have inscribed these intentions. The simple process of voicing their new goals will have already made their intended change more concrete.

The Camera Never Blinks

What stories do you remember about one female relative or another that entice or inspire you? Even if you are reading this book on your own, try to find a way to share these tales with a group of friends. Talking together often pushes your mind down unpredictable paths of discovery and memory. However you proceed, I trust that you will find that looking backward in order to move forward makes you realize that you do indeed have sturdy roots.

Now find as many childhood pictures of yourself as you can, pictures ranging from infancy through teenage years if possible. Then study your development. Notice your appearance, mood, and any significant changes. It helps to lay the pictures out across a flat surface in some manner of chronological order. Take as long as you need to work through the following questions. You may choose to look first at relatives and later at pictures from your own childhood. The important thing is to let your memory work off of the pictures—let the visual record prompt your thoughts to roam.

As you study the pictures, ask and answer the following questions:

- What do you see in your childhood face? Do you see someone who is happy and carefree, or someone who is sad? Are you performing in the pictures, or hiding?

- Where and in what situations do you look natural and where do you look posed?

- Are there any marked changes in your looks or behavior? How did your hair change? How did your choice of clothing change? Who are you with in the pictures?

- What life experiences do you remember that accompanied each of the marked changes? Did you move, were you on vacation, was something happening to the family, were you simply becoming a teen or an adult?

- In conclusion, review how and when you got off your "individual track" and onto the track society encouraged. When did you begin to play the roles that were expected of you?

Now look back even further, at pictures of parents, grandparents, great-grandparents, aunts, and cousins. As above, let the pictures stimulate your memories.

- What stories do you remember about these relatives and how they lived their lives?

- What impact did each of these relatives have on your life?

- Do you look like one or another of your kin? Did you take on some of her personality quirks?

- From what you remember, what were some of her outstanding characteristics? Have you ever considered emulating her?

Finally, make a list of these outstanding characteristics and find someplace highly visible to put it. Choose one enticing quality each week, and begin to emulate your relative.

This exercise is meant to encourage you to look as far backward as you can, both to understand your own ache and to retrieve some of the characteristics embedded within your gene pool that you might consider strengths. Once you have identified the power of your relative ability, you can begin to draw on it regularly. After all, there is no point in limiting your way of being yourself.

Life Cycle Logic

My appreciation of my relative ability sustained me for quite a time, and I felt myself break free from many of the constraints of my old ways of looking at myself. But it wasn't until I began working through the stages of my life cycle with Joan Erikson that I truly understood how much I, myself, had to offer. Joan prodded and poked me onto new paths from the moment I met her, and early on I had begun to include her in my reserve of relative ability. Then, one day, she suggested I go a little further. "You know, dear," she began, "you've made great strides as a result of cultivating the characteristics that you have inherited from your various relatives, but it's time you looked at the many strengths you have developed on your own. We all need to see and feel our independent power, to search for our life's meaning, and learn that it is all in here," she said pointing to her heart. "When we realize this, we no longer need to look outward for affirmation. We can simply begin to sponsor ourselves!"

I have since thought how fortuitous that I ran into the Eriksons rather than Freud or Jung. I suspect that Freud would have analyzed me on his couch for a good ten years, reviewing all of my weaknesses, and Jung would have had me turning over rock after rock in search of my shadow side. Joan Erikson, on the other hand, helped me to see that I could derive fresh energy and strength as I tried to reinvent and reinvigorate myself by looking closely at how I had managed the roadblocks, obstacles, and challenging crossroads of my life, at those places and times when I'd made the right decision, stayed the course, hung on, avoided the pitfalls, or simply crawled out of a hole after falling in. She explained that strength comes from adversity, and that new energy is generated from the tensions with which we are made to work. Using her husband's famous psychoanalytic theories as a rough guide, Joan encouraged me to review my life, focusing on what I did to succeed rather than, as was my tendency, on how I had failed.

In order to thrive, not simply to survive, you must understand your life cycle. Look over the Eriksons' eight stages and the strengths that accompany each one. As you remember specific times in your childhood or adulthood, think about how by resolving certain conflicts you earned one or more of these strengths. Recognizing your weaknesses and identifying your powers are also ways to reclaim your selfhood.

INFANCY:	Trust versus Mistrust; the strength gained is HOPE
EARLY CHILDHOOD:	Autonomy versus Shame; the strength gained is WILL
PLAY AGE:	Initiative versus Guilt; the strength gained is PURPOSE
SCHOOL AGE:	Industry versus Inferiority; the strength gained is COMPETENCE
ADOLESCENCE:	Identity versus Confusion; the strength gained is FIDELITY
YOUNG ADULTHOOD:	Intimacy versus Isolation; the strength gained is LOVE

| ADULTHOOD: | Generativity versus Stagnation; the strength gained is CARE |
| OLD AGE: | Integrity versus Despair; the strength gained is WISDOM |

List the gains and losses that you can remember in each stage of your life. Focus on your successes—how you worked your way around obstacles or out of conflicts. Then try to identify the innate strengths you brought to each situation. Make a list of these strengths. They are yours to be used again and again.

The Colors of Your Life

Because Joan's manner was always to show, not tell, we did most of our talking about our pasts while weaving tapestries of our individual life cycles on small looms. Joan had developed her own theory that each of the stages could be represented by a single color. She chose *light blue* for *hope; orange* for *will; green* for *purpose; yellow* for *competence; dark blue* for *fidelity; red* for *love; light green* for *care;* and *purple* for *wisdom.* We wove a stripe for each stage and added splashes of additional yarn as we talked about the experiences that had "colored" our lives. "I have always thought of the self as a richly colored tapestry," Joan told me, "with each thread significant to the integrity of the whole design. Layers of history and circumstances have made us one way, but it is important to peel off the layers and find all the buried parts of you. The root growing in the dry ground is the one we're after, dear."

While weaving with Joan, I learned that each of us is who she is because of a unique mix of experience. Joan's tapestry looked nothing like mine—her colors were wilder and more abundant, mine somewhat safe and more predictably layered, and she all but covered up her loom while I still had a third of the warp left to fill with all the color I wanted. The colorful, unfinished tapestry affirmed my growing conviction that I had all the raw material for change available to me and brought to life the words of one of my favorite writers, Florida Scott-Maxwell: "You need only to claim the events of your life to make yourself yours." And so it was that I became fierce about my future and the futures of the women I know. A colorful life is within all of our grasps.

Later, I took the colors from my weaving and braided them into a strand that I tucked into my purse, where I could finger it frequently. These pieces of thread have become a sort of lifeline for me—a palpable reminder of my striving.

Now that you have a greater grasp of your struggles and your strengths, why not braid the colors of your life together? Note the colors that Joan Erikson chose to represent the eight stages.

- Lay out strands of yarn or embroidery thread to represent each stage.

- Think about your greatest strengths, and choose many threads of that color.

- Continue through the strengths for each stage, picking up an appropriate amount of color to represent the presence of that strength in your own life.

- When you have a bundle of eight colors, add some hot pink or chartreuse green to represent fun, vibrant, wild times. Add some browns and blacks for the more somber moments.

It is easiest to do the actual braiding with a partner, as the women do on the weekend retreats. As your partner holds one end of your bundle, begin to braid the colors of your life together, telling your story and explaining why you are using more of one color than another. You are working against a lifetime of ingrained habit when you try to focus on your strengths, rather than your wounds. Sometimes it takes outside eyes and ears, as well as understanding and affirmation, for us to see that all the hardship and loss have prepared us to reclaim our lives.

Lorraine, a retreater from Arizona wrote to me:

The braiding was very difficult for me. It was so much easier to make observations about the woman I was working with on the braid than to look at myself. When I first went up to the table to pick out my strands of yarn, I couldn't even decide how much to take of any one color. I remember I looked around and started to follow what another woman was doing. Instinctively it felt wrong, but I needed my partner to literally guide me through. Once we started braiding, the stories came easily enough. I was able to share stories from each of the eight stages, but they were all pretty horrible. I had to talk about being raped as a child, dropping out of school, my parent's divorce, and my son's drug addiction. I felt like crying, not weaving! Then Beverly reached across the yarn and held my hand. "What strength of will you have developed," she said. I had never seen that strength in myself. To me, it was a survival instinct based on fear and a feeling of vulnerability. But I felt so proud when she observed strength of will. And I realized that my life has been shaped by an amazing will to accomplish and survive. I got up and grabbed a whole lot of orange yarn. I take out my braided strand every now and then, I see all that orange. It makes me feel strong. I know, too, when I look at it that I do have more strengths that I can uncover if I continue to look for them rather than drown in the memory of trouble. I fully intend to braid some more ropes, and I know that pretty soon I'll have a wall-full of color.

As one color blends with another, metaphorically you will reconstruct the span of your life. Go back over your braid as many times as you want, never undoing the knot at the top, but adding color as memories spring forth—an unfinished, evolving life symbolized in living colors!

We already possess everything we need to move forward. Each of us has inherited all the bold vision, the courage, the compassion, and the integrity to repair our lives and spirits. These sturdy roots may have been neglected and hidden under years of accumulated dirt, misunderstanding, and social conformity, but they have not withered. It is our job to reach down, retrieve the strengths that are our birthright, and wrest them out into the light. We live in a culture that tells us we can make ourselves new by changing our shape, face, or place of residence. But these are only externals, superficial improvements that do little to connect us to anything solid or sustaining. Real change comes with time and involves the arduous work of recalling our history, without which we can never recover ourselves.

We are all so very unique. What a precious gift the world loses if we don't find out who we are and then share our individuality.

END OF CHAPTER SUMMARY

- Celebrate your roots
- Draw on your relative ability

- Study your life cycle
- Choose the colors for your life
- Make a new creation out of the old self
- Declare an intention

Intentions

The word *intention* comes from the Latin root *intendere,* meaning "to stretch toward something." It is important for any woman in need of changing direction, personality, and attitude to form an intention or a series of intentions so that she will stretch toward a new way of being. I formed my first set of intentions when I wrote down all of the qualities I admired in my female relatives. This list gave me something to reach for and a sense of direction. Later, when I convinced a fisherman to take me out to see the seals, I came up with another series of intentions.

At first I couldn't understand what it was that made the seals so special. They were fat, and brown and gray, and they barked. But I was entranced as I watched their antics. After a while, it dawned on me that they were behaving in a way that I would like to behave. They were playful, in the moment, vulnerable, undomesticated, mysterious, curious, mischievous, fun, and at home in their bodies.

I reached around in my backpack and found an old receipt on which I quickly penciled all of the attributes and attitudes that I found so delightful. Back on shore, I taped this list up on the bathroom mirror, where I saw it first thing every morning. As with the list I formed while looking through the photo albums, this one kept me focused on who I wanted to be and how I wanted to live my life.

Writing down a word or a series of words that delight you and remind you of who you could be is an important first step toward repair and change. Forming a series of intentions, or just identifying one intention, will help you stake a claim on which new path you want to pursue. It will give you direction and a goal.

The most important thing is to remember that intentions are pure possibilities. They are entitlements as well as wishes that can overshadow any limitation or previous way of behaving. Even so, intentions are gentle and never forced. They are resolutions without the determined edge—dreams of what could be—they are different and exciting.

Intentions can be a new way to embrace life—a positive attitude, a series of wild characteristics previously thought to be forbidden or unattainable. They can be one word each, or a series of words strung together. They come from noticing characteristics or qualities that appeal to you, just as I did after observing the seals. They can be verbs, nouns, or adjectives; attitudes, actions, or feelings. An intention can even be a color.

What words come to mind? *Resilient, determined, wild, free, silly.* Or perhaps *wild, salty, impetuous, buoyant, fun, naughty,* or *vulnerable*? After you have covered an entire page with descriptive words, circle the ones you are drawn to—the ones that you perhaps have longed to project or be. Most likely this is how you were as a rebellious adolescent or an impetuous child, until such behavior was simply beaten out of you. The sooner you name some intentions, the sooner you will begin walking the road back, not only to the raw-material person you once were, but toward the strength you inherently possess to shift and change.

CRAZY QUILT

Another illuminating sharing exercise to do with other women is to make a crazy quilt. Each woman brings to the meeting scraps of fabric, pieces of old clothing, bits of yarn, lace, mementos, slogans—anything that is a reminder of both the turbulent and the wonderful times of her life. Sitting around a big table, each woman creates her own square or section by patching together these scraps. As you patch, share the stories behind each piece. When everyone has finished her separate piece, pin them all onto a large cloth sheet. The quilt can now be used as a centerpiece at gatherings, as a wall hanging, as something that gets passed around the group.

Clarissa Pinkola Estes believes that, "to work in organic matter, one simplifies, stays more toward sensing and feeling, rather than intellectualization. Sometimes it is helpful, as one of my late colleagues use to say—to think in terms that would be understood by a bright ten year old." She continues, explaining that throughout Mesoamerica spinning and weaving of cloth were ways to invite or be informed by the spirit. "There is serious evidence that the making of thread and cloth were once religious practices used to teach the cycles of life and death and beyond."

The crazy quilt is an exercise to help us look backward and own all that we have endured and worked through. It is a liberating exercise, one meant to strengthen and support us "carriers of culture."

Repair Body and Soul

Turn Up the Silence,
Turn Down the Voices

*"After a certain point, it is necessary to let go of all
outside help and focus in on our own strength and re-
sourcefulness. What we seek, seeks us."*

ANONYMOUS

Seize Your Day

"This is a moon-shell day," I tell the group of retreaters who
have gathered in the living room of our little inn early on
Saturday morning. I hold up the rounded shell that is in the
palm of my hand. "This is a day to spiral inward, just as this
snail shell does—to be self-contained and serene—to write
your own prescriptions and find your center. It is a day of
silence and solitude when you will go from being alone to
being all one."

I am always excited about the Saturday portion of the
weekend program, because I always yearn for the same si-

lence, solitude, and focus that I offer to these women. I also crave the remoteness of the barrier beach we are about to hike and the physical strenuousness of the adventure. As I look around the room, I see that the women have done what they can to prepare themselves for the day's sandy, five-mile walk. They're all wearing comfortable clothing, sturdy shoes, hats or visors, and lot of layers. But I know that, despite the appropriateness of their gear, very few are mentally prepared for what they will experience when the boat drops them off at the outermost tip of South Beach—a fifty-yard-wide arm of sand that reaches five miles out into the Atlantic Ocean.

Once we have finished our morning discussion, we will walk a mile down to the little harbor and board two small boats, be motored out to see the seals at Monomoy Island, and then be dropped for our solo hike. For the better part of the day, everyone will be on her own in an unfamiliar natural environment. So, over breakfast, I try to lay the mental and emotional groundwork for the day.

"We have done enough aching; we understand the importance of retreat; we have worked to retrieve ourselves and garner our strengths from the past. Today is about repair—it's about turning 'alone' into 'all one.' It is about pushing beyond the limits we put on ourselves and experiencing what it feels like to be a tidal woman—someone who welcomes the highs and lows, who looks beneath the sand, rides the waves, and stays in the flow of life. The fundamental thing about the journey, as Anne Morrow Lindbergh once said, is that we women must come of age by ourselves. We must find our true centers alone. That is why today's walk is meant to be a solo experience. Resist the urge to walk with a friend or stop to talk. When you allow yourself to be alone, truly alone, without other people limiting your thoughts, feelings, and responses, unexpected insights and desires spring into the light and take hold. Seize them—for once there will be no one around to stop you. What I hope for you today is that, as you turn up the silence and turn off the voices, you will experience a wildness that you will never again want to be without."

I stare at a sea of puzzled faces and try a new tack. "I sense anxiety coming from some of you. Perhaps you feel you haven't trained enough, your knees are weak, you fear isolation. But I know that you've come here to be tested and to try something new. As Joan Erikson said to me, 'When you are alone, you find out who you are capable of being.' You find out how far you can stretch, reach, and escape, all the while coming to know what's fun and what gives you satisfaction. This is your time to stretch and escape."

I know the women hear only half of what I say. The majority of them can't let go of some nagging concern or another. Without realizing it, most of them are just plain nervous about the solitude and lack of structure. Sure enough, as soon as I stop talking, hands go up all over the room. The women want more practical details. "Could you draw me a map of the area?" "Will the boat be in rough seas?" "How do we keep from getting disoriented . . . especially in this fog?" "How long should the hike take?" Some have already confessed to a dread of the water—that they've never learned to swim, or that they suffer from seasickness. I reflect back to my journey along the Inca Trail and tell them about the full-blown anxiety attack I experienced at the beginning of the trek. As I realized later, my fear was all about venturing into the unknown and being made to relinquish control.

Poet May Sarton had a fear of adventure and isolation as well, I say. Her need to be alone was always balanced against her fear of what might happen when suddenly she entered the huge empty silence and found no support. Because we women so often plan the adventures, we have trouble trusting anyone else's plans for us. "Embracing the abundant freedom you are about to experience is frightening as well as exciting. But think about it. The root word for adventure is *advent,* which means *beginning,* and with every beginning there is bound to be anxiety. Acknowledge your anxiety, but keep your sights focused on the adventure. I promise you that your reward will be myriad intoxicating experiences that will only whet your appetite for more."

This part of the retreat arose out of a very specific experience I had a few years back. "For those of you who are extraordinarily wounded," I continue, "it's so hard to get rid of the anger and resist pointing the finger. But anger only serves to take you away from yourself. This walk is meant to bring you back to yourself, as it did for me.

"One day I found some nasty letters my brother wrote to our mother in which he berated me over and over. Burning with anger and a sense of injustice, I went for a long walk on this very beach. With every stride, I found myself saying, 'Damn him! How could he?' He had gotten to my core, and I was filled with his venom. Here I was in my favorite place, pounding the sand with my feet, and I felt shadowed, haunted, and utterly estranged, even from myself. Finally, I fell to my knees, screaming to the wind: 'God. Give me a sign that you are with me—that I have done nothing wrong.' I paused and listened, hoping for an answer. Just then a seal popped its head up out of the waves directly in front of me—then two more appeared. I stared at them and they stared back at me, and then a gentle rain began to fall. Instead of grabbing for my parka, I let the warm drops bathe my body. I felt blessed—baptized, even—certainly protected and held by something larger than myself. I had been taken beyond my angry issues. Suddenly my brother and his anger were washed away with the tide, and I found myself smiling—smiling from a sense of peace and the spirit of the seals.

"Later, as I processed what had actually occurred, I came to see that I had been in that 'I want' place again, rather than the 'I am.' I had wanted him to recognize and admit that I was a good person. I wanted him not to write those crappy letters. I wanted his thoughts and feelings to change. But I couldn't do anything about *his* feelings, the letters, or anything else. In the rain, with the seals, I was able to return to the 'I am' place. Yes, I am sad. I am hurt. I am tired. I am wet. But I am also a good, caring person, and that is what matters.

"My hope for you today is that you will find a similar grace and blessing in this remote and natural place. Like most women, South Beach has its own history of breakage and repair. It used to be part of a long stretch of barrier beach that protected the entire harbor of Chatham. But in 1987 a powerful nor'easter broke through and split the beach in half. For a time the town and its inhabitants were vulnerable. But no longer. Like a strong woman, the beach managed to endure, each winter adding depth and width to her girth. Over time, small dunes have risen up, creating shelter for all manner of wildlife, and, today, shelter for you.

"When you finally disembark from the boat and stand at the tip of the beach, you will feel as though you've landed on the moon; there are no signs of human activity or society; no vegetation taller than your hip; and the sea, sand, and sky melt into each other. Just as this beach was rejuvenated, so I hope you will be also.

"Once on shore, find a spot that calls to you. Create

your space. Give in to the solitude and the vastness, and let go of control. Sink into the seamless world of uninterrupted time, where the endless hours allow something to grow from nothing. Gather yourself up and hold her tight. Let solitude begin the repair. Some of you will be drawn to the pounding surf, others will crave the stillness of the protected bay, and then there are those of you who will choose to walk straight down the middle, pushing your way through the tall, spiky beach grass, gazing at the conflicting vistas.

"Last October, Terri from New Jersey simply got off the boat, headed for the nearest dune, and took a two-hour nap. On that same retreat, Marcia, after being captivated by the playfulness of the seals, wanted to be naked and free. The first one out of the boat, Marcia hightailed it toward the tip of the peninsula, where a few seals had gathered. She ceremoniously removed her clothes and piled them neatly in the sand. Then, clasping her hands above her head, she dove in for a swim. Later, she admitted that she almost didn't do it, not because she was afraid of the fifty-four-degree water, but because she felt guilty that her intrusion into the seals' pod would cause them to scatter, thus ruining the other women's chance to enjoy them. But she caught herself, knowing that she came on this weekend to stop her incessant worrying about others. She needed to leap—to have an experience just for her—and it was worth it."

Empty Out

"Today you are to go to a place where there are few limitations—where the dome of sky meets the dancing sea, where the environment as well as the day is limitless. That's the good news. The bad news is that, in order to get the most out of the moment, you will need not maps and timetables but to lighten your load. 'You can't possibly climb up the mountain to a new life without unloading your knapsack of all the heavy stuff that has been weighing you down,' Joan Erikson cautioned me. 'It's best to travel light and dump the unnecessary baggage.'

"During her lifetime, Joan managed to dump things such as: regrets, judgments, Harvard, tight suits, nylon stockings, depression, organized religion, and perfection. Each time she dumped something, she made more room in her life for the joie de vivre she chased.

"We must empty out in order to put our high-gear personalities into slow motion. 'Make yourself empty so the great soul of the universe can fill you with its breath,' said writer Laurence Binyon. During my year by the sea, I methodically 'cleaned house.' I got rid of such things as: toxic relationships, stultifying routines, dead weight, extra pounds, ambivalence, and people-pleasing. Now every weekend program includes some time for the dumping of baggage and agendas.

"Last fall, fifty-two-year-old Mary Ann decided to bury the sunglasses that had been her cover for the past twenty years; thirty-eight-year-old Lucy filled snail shells with the names of people she no longer needed or wanted in her life and tossed them, one by one, into the sea; forty-five-year-old Joyce Ann had had enough of feeling enslaved to fluctuating numbers, so she stuffed her bathroom scale into her knapsack, lugged it onto the outer beach, and ceremoniously buried it in a large dune; Pat dropped her cancer-survivor pin overboard, because she wanted to be seen as more than just a survivor; together Rebecca and Amy threw their wedding rings up in the air and out of sight; forty-one-year-old Jane buried a photograph of herself, her husband, and her best friend with whom he'd had an affair; and workaholic Barbara buried last year's overpacked daybook and resolved to quit the corporate world and go into business for herself.

"Now it is your turn. Take half an hour to conduct an inventory of what you need to rid from your life. The following questions will help guide you."

Lighten Your Load

· What baggage have you been dying to get rid of?

· How could you lighten your "psychic load"? In other words, what obligations, "should" activities, responsibilities, or negative pressures can you dump?

- Who in your life should not be there anymore?
- What negative voices would you like to silence, whether they are echoes from your past or voices in your present?

This exercise is key to repair—you must create a blank palette and begin to make space for what really matters in your day and in your life. I encourage you to follow Lucy's lead and make a ceremony out of the exercise. Build a fire, and toss your list into the flames; tear your list into shreds and flush it down the toilet; scatter birdseed at the park and mentally toss your list up into the air as well; go to the dump with a bag of bottles and deliberately toss them out one by one. The important thing is to commit yourself to throwing out your psychic baggage.

Serendipity

And so another beach walk commences. There is the last-minute flurry as the women grab extra water bottles, run to the bathroom, and then head out for the mile hike to our waiting boats. The murky gray day is perfect—a blank canvas or Joan Erikson's empty loom waiting to be filled.

The little voyage, which usually takes fifteen minutes, will take twice that today, thanks to the heavy fog. But mysterious circumstances only serve to enhance an adventure, I remind myself. I lean back in my seat and let the comforting, misty air touch my face, its moisture a cool drink for my dry skin. All is well, as I gaze around at the expectant faces, and I am supremely confident that this experience and today's trek will penetrate even the most hardened souls.

Suddenly I hear a gasp—heads turn toward starboard, and the magic begins—a full pod of seals are treading water, welcoming us into their space! Their presence sends a charge through the boats full of women, most of whom sit hushed and still. It has been said that simply gazing into a seal's eyes makes something eternal happen. The seals clued me in to what was missing in my life—things like vulnerability, being at home in my body, playfulness, mystery, undomestication, to name a few. I am always curious about what the women I take with me on these voyages will find. Although the captain of our little boat shares some basic information about these enchanting creatures, we all know that this is a spiritual journey, not an Audubon field trip.

The seals' energy is immediately contagious. They are seductive, tempting each of us to dive in and swim. At the very least, their innocent, unguarded curiosity and playfulness always make me feel open and ready for the remainder of the day. Other wild creatures add to the production. Several gulls swoop down, battling for the same fish, as a flock of cormorants takes flight from a nearby sandbar, and a round ball of sun pops through the moving clouds and offers momentary clarity. There is promise that light is around the bend, and we all strain for a glimpse of our final destination.

As we head for the tip of South Beach, the women are primed for whatever will come next—primed for everything, that is, except our landing. I had warned them that they would be getting their feet wet (in more ways than one), but a few women seem surprised when I tell them to take off their shoes and roll up their pants. As the boat edges into the sand, they haul their bodies overboard and rush some twenty-five feet in frigid water toward shore, fortunately laughing all the way.

Once on dry land, they move off into the mist—shoulders dropped, eyes open wide, smiles softening previously anxious or stern faces. I am confident they will find their places on this landscape—this barren beach upon which they can write their hopes and dreams. "Grow a new attitude," I whisper. "See how invigorating life can be when there are no limits."

One thing I know, there will be tears. One past retreater named Marilyn didn't think she needed the weekend, but she came anyway at her friend's urging. She began her walk with determination and speed, just as she always did on her favorite beach back on Long Island. Suddenly she heard the soft voice of her mother, who had been dead for fifteen years. "There, there," the voice said. "Slow down. Be still. You are moving too fast. You don't have to do it all. There, there."

Marilyn stopped in her tracks. Up until then, she had been intent only on getting the damn hike over with, but after the unexpected intrusion, her body began to melt. All the stress she had left behind—a daughter's upcoming wedding, another daughter's troubled pregnancy, and a husband fighting open-heart surgery—slipped away. Perhaps her mother was assuring her that she was meant to be here after all. Marilyn stumbled to a nearby log, sat down, and let herself sob. She had never had the time to grieve her mother's passing. In fact, she hadn't had time for feeling anything much—until now.

Another retreater, forty-five-year-old Cathy, was also gifted with tears on her beach walk.

It was so foggy that it became difficult to see. Yet the fog was perfect. It was how I had lived my life—lost in the fog. But today I was not lost. This time I had a destination—a path. Each step forward was one more step away from the past with all of its accompanying masks and fears. I left as much sadness as I could in each footprint I made in the sand, pressing down hard to make a deep imprint. As I was walking, I found a fish bone in the likeness of a mask. I said over and over again that masks are no longer for me. That's when the tears began to flow, and in the silence I heard my voice say, "It's OK, let it go, Cathy, just let it all go." And then it seemed that the healing began. The lighthouse appeared in the distance to guide me back.

Still others will be overcome with giddiness, like Maria.

After I heard Joan say that I would never get this particular day back again, I decided to make the most of it—to see how long I could stretch out the time. Instead of pushing toward the finish, I lingered, slept, swam, wrote, played, drew pictures, and eventually made the most incredible mermaid in the sand, complete with seaweed hair, big boobs, and a jingly shell necklace. I hadn't built anything in the sand since I was a child. I reveled in the ease with which the sand slipped through my fingers, and then suddenly I had this gorgeous free woman beside me—I made her, just like I was remaking me. I took a picture of my sculpture and began heading back, feeling lighter with each step. Time had stopped—and that was big. I didn't realize how big until I walked back into the inn and everyone was having cocktails! Where have you been? they wondered. My reply: I just had the best day of my life.

What will be the stories from this group, I wonder? Serendipity will work its magic. New impulses will surface, and the process of repair will have commenced.

Gifts from the Sea

Five hours later, I sit on the porch of the inn and await the women's return. One after another appears at the end of the street, slowly making her way toward me. Some seem under a spell, others bedraggled, still others light and high, almost. Their arms are full of debris—such things as buoys, oddly shaped pieces of driftwood, fishline, and rope. God only knows what else will be dumped out of their backpacks. Their faces are sweaty and windburned, their eyes are glassy with dreams or sparkling with fire. I wave, and they quicken their steps, hungry for the brown-bag lunches that are piled nearby. And then, as they gobble their sandwiches, they begin to babble about the day, the place, the soft sand, and the waves. They unload their packs, reaching for tattered journals, a shell or a rock from which they have garnered meaning. They are amazed at their poetry, their original thoughts, the "aha" moments that came, one after another. Once the majority of the women are back, we recall the drama of the day.

"Well, today's walk was different, even for me," I admit. "Out there, on the freezing, foggy point, I became very disoriented, even anxious. And then I thought: How wonderful. What a great experience for careful women. Somehow we all think we have to save ourselves for our children, our family—we're trained to be so cautious. It is good, after all, to be disoriented and forced out of our comfort zone."

None of the women disagree. "So that's what I found today. How about you?"

Susan from California speaks first.

I have erected so many defenses against myself, but today, on the beach, my walls melted away. I felt alone and yet not lonely. There was no one to justify myself to and no one to carry along. It was just me, and it was extraordinary.

Bethany from Michigan speaks next.

I brought back these three shells. The first one was large and circular, and when I saw it, I thought of the moon shell Joan held up this morning. I was so happy, because I felt that I had found the perfect sign. But when I picked it up out of the sand, I saw that it was broken and jagged and not at all like Joan's. Then I saw a sturdy clamshell. I wanted that shell because it had so much strength. But when I picked it up, it came unhinged right in my hands. Finally, I saw this last shell. It is so ordinary on the outside—just mottled grey and bumpy. But when you turn it over, it is filled with color and shimmers. I knew then that I had gotten my message. I need to turn myself inside out, find my colorful, shimmering underlayer, and revel in its beauty. I need a new way of looking at myself, imperfect and perfect.

Then Gail.

I retrieved a shell, too, that when I first saw it, I thought: How beautiful and perfect. Which is what I thought my husband, Brian, was. I did not like me, and I hadn't for years. But I thought he was perfect. Even after he left me, I still thought he was perfect. When I picked up this shell, I saw that it had a big hole in it. And so I thought, Brian is not perfect. I walked along with my shell for a while, until I suddenly realized: I don't want to be carrying Brian with me. But when I went to toss the shell away, my arm went limp and it fell at my feet. That's when I realized that the problem was not with the shell, or even with Brian, for that matter. My problem was that when I saw the shell I thought of him and not of myself. I came to the realization that letting go meant seeing reflections of myself in the world around me, rather than always signs of him. So I picked up the shell and brought it home to remind me that I can be as beautiful as this shell, even with all of my flaws.

Jungian analyst Marion Woodman once wrote, "Our bodies love metaphors because they join our bodies to our souls rather than abandoning them to a soulless state." I am amazed at how easily the women are demonstrating the truth behind this statement, and at how easily they seem to have responded to the beach. Their stories keep coming.

Colleen, one of the women who almost did not do the walk, shares her triumph with the group.

I went and stood by the water's edge at first. I just prayed, and I felt this power coming in to help me do what I really wanted to do—the whole walk. I walked alone for quite a while, just happy to be on my way and determined not to give up. But I was also still afraid that I wouldn't make it, that I'd die in the dunes all alone. Then I found these three connected buoys. This is my lifeline, I said to myself. So I picked them up and carried them with me the whole way home. I dragged these buoys behind me, and I felt that I was strong. I thought, Look at me, I am carrying my own lifeline for myself. At one point, I was pretty wet and cold and the buoys felt heavy. I was tempted to let them go, and I could feel myself getting discouraged. But then I heard this woman laughing. Jill came up beside me, and she was just laughing out loud to herself. She said she had been follow-ing my trail in the sand. She offered to help me drag the buoys, and I suddenly knew that I could do it on my own. Jill walked ahead, and I followed her laughter all the way home.

Sonya found a sign in a piece of rope.

It was all tangled up in a knot, and I thought to myself, Well, it's all tangled up, just like I am. It has too much in-frastructure.

Deborah looked up at the birds.

I noticed that the gulls face the wind, they don't turn their backs on difficulty, and as a result, they use the wind to lift them higher and send them farther.

Eileen exchanged her grief for shells.

I got out of the boat and I said to myself, "I am going to do this whole walk, and I will not feel guilt for anyone." And I walked and I walked without stopping. But guilt is habitual for me, and pretty soon I slipped into the mode of "No shell shall be left behind." So my bag got heavier and heavier. I got soup-bowl-size shells initially, then, slowly, smaller and smaller ones, as I ran out of room. Eventually I had to stop. I had to stop and let go of the shells. It was really hard. I stood there for a while and marveled at how I came to dump my guilt, and here I stood feeling guilty for leaving behind a shell. That made me see how ridiculous I was being. So I made a ritual out of letting go. I dragged my bag to the shoreline and tossed the shells by the handful into each wave just as it broke against the sand. I returned with an empty bag and no guilt. I feel like a new woman!

One woman after another speaks of a breakthrough—just as the beach itself was broken at one point, creating a channel through which they had to wade. It was an unexpected occurrence, something that had happened during a recent storm and that I hadn't prepared them for. Many women saw it as a sign—that they were now ready to welcome the unexpected, that true life indeed happens outside of what we have planned or imagined even, and that was what had made the beach walk so exhilarating. Carla watched the water turn itself around in this channel and felt her own thoughts change.

For the whole first half of the walk, I was living a fantasy. I felt that I was walking away from my life. Then I came to the channel, and I watched the water turn back on itself. I realized that I was walking back toward my life. I stopped and sat there for a while, until I had my head around that idea, until I knew if that was the direction I wanted to go. When I was ready, I stood up and trudged purposefully toward the lighthouse.

As the talk continues and the sun begins to set, it is clear that, by daring to walk beyond their old limits, the women had learned much about themselves. I reach for the easel to write the new set of rules these women would begin to in-corporate into their lives—"lifelines for change," I call them. *Take action. Have an adventure. Face your fear. Seize the moment. Tolerate isolation. Reach beyond your grasp.*

I can't begin to count the number of times skeptics have challenged me: "How could all of that happen in a mere five hours?" My answer: "It's amazing what can happen to a woman if she can only find personal time." The experience of embark-ing on a solitary excursion, no matter how grand or how small, in a remote, unfamiliar, natural place, can't help but create a range of emotions, new incentives, and original thoughts.

What's more, the experience stays with the women.

Many retreaters have written to tell me how the effects of the walk continue to influence them.

I returned home from my weekend changed. I felt more confident, somehow. But it was even more than that. It was like a part of me had been awakened after a long deep sleep. Up until then, I had been scattered, strewn about. Pieces of me—wife, mother, daughter, friend—were all there, but there were also gaping holes. Where were the missing pieces? That was scary to me because what would those pieces be like if and when I found them. More than that, were there any pieces to find?

On the walk I had to talk myself into relaxing. I was cold, disoriented, scattered, and the damn lighthouse seemed too far away. But then I developed this never say die attitude—the tide pulled back from the shore and the sand became firm and I found a comfortable gait and took off. I came to see that whatever bump was in the road I could get around it.

We are not, nor should we ever be mere bits and pieces, and yet we never seem to make the time to find the missing pieces or connect the dots like we did when we were kids in those fun activity books. How much fun it was to see a blank page of dots and when we were finished have a total picture. The beach walk allowed me to connect the dots. For certain I found several vital missing pieces to my puz-

zle. I went home determined to finish the job no matter how long I had to search or how hard I had to work.

And so, as we sip our wine and watch the sunset paint the open sky, I raise my glass to these pilgrims: "You have crossed a threshold and are on the road to a more abundant life."

A Scavenger Hunt for Your Soul

A psychiatrist once told me that it was impossible to stay depressed while being active. The monk Thomas Merton had a variation on the same theme when he suggested, "You can't be neurotic in front of a bunch of trees." Indeed, I have long since come to know that nature feeds a woman's soul. It rarely gives direct answers, but it always nourishes, soothes, and waters the spirit, so that eventually growth occurs.

Strong, silent, natural places have a way of smoothing our rough edges. In the forest, on a mesa, beside a pond, beneath a waterfall, on top of a mountain, confusion, rage, and sorrow all but disappear. "To the mind that is still," said Lao Tzu, "the whole universe surrenders."

Where would you go for an extended solo sojourn in nature? Try to think of an environment that is as natural, unfamiliar, and unbounded as possible. It is preferable if you have never been there before, and if you've not done anything like it as well. Your sojourn need not be physically grueling, but it must take you out of your milieu for a time. I suggest that you plan to be away and active for at least four hours. You need to give yourself time to truly experience a beginning, a middle, and an end. There are no shortcuts in soul work. You must take the time to stumble and pick yourself up, to rest before pushing on, to sit under the tree, to take time in a cave before coming back into the light. The journey's strength is always realized in the middle, when your body is tired, the elements are their harshest, and you hope for rescue. As Joan Erikson would say, "The struggle, the pull and the tug, are everything."

Would you go on a desert path up to a mesa? a section of a well-known trail? a daylong cross-country ski? a kayaking voyage or portaging adventure? an overnight camping trip? As with the beach walk, push yourself to go on your own. If you go with a friend, make sure you have at least two hours in solitude. The more time you take alone, the better. On your sojourn, let your spirit go. Walk, run, meander, connect to the environment, and savor the silence. If an idea or an object bumps into you, follows you, find out what it has to offer. These serendipitous exchanges will raise your passion for living.

Before you leave, pack a journal. Tuck inside its pages this list of things to look for as a way of settling into your chosen environment. Once you are comfortable on your sojourn, pull out the journal and conduct a scavenger hunt for your soul. Look for:

- An object that is finished
- A stone that speaks
- A sound that stirs
- An unexpected sight
- Something that is alive
- An object that holds another object

Think about each item you find. What can it tell you about your life, your feelings, your goals? The scavenger hunt is designed to keep you focused on the moment as well as the environment at hand, and to distract you when the physicality of the day begins to overpower.

Sit with your thoughts before returning to others.

Navajo Vision Quest

Many Native Americans, in order to get in touch with their inner selves, go away from the pueblo, out into the wilderness for a vision quest. They find a spot that speaks to them, collect stones to create a circular border, and then sit in the center of their circle for twenty-four hours to hear what their heart, or the Great Spirit, needs to tell them.

Something about the discipline of taking time to be away and focused without any distraction attracted me to do a modified version of a "vision quest" during my year by the sea. I found a wonderful spot in a remote section of my local beach. It had a piling to lean against, and I got in the habit of frequenting it once a week. At dawn on the designated date, I walk slowly to my spot, collect shells along the way, and place them in a circle near the piling. Once inside "my space," sitting with my legs crossed, I sit for some thirty minutes, listening to my breathing, and then breathing rhythmically with the ocean, tuning out thoughts while welcoming and focusing on sounds and smells. Within ten minutes or less, my attention is always drawn to a word, an intention, an inclination, or something else that gives meaning to my day and ensuing week. After being lost in this psychic space, I come away refreshed and spiritually informed.

I suggest this exercise to the women on retreat as a way to get centered before embarking on the beach walk. One woman confessed to me that it is hard for her to sit still, and that when she is presented with a place such as a beach, she finds it very hard not to walk. Still, she heeded my advice, drew a circle in the sand, and sat in the middle of it. For the first time in a long while, she felt secure in her own space, protected from others by the boundary she had drawn in the sand, and she was able to focus like never before.

As we continue to understand that true knowledge can

only come from within, the "vision quest" is one way to ensure that we will stay on the course.

END OF CHAPTER SUMMARY

- Lighten your load
- Have a solo adventure
- Accept nature's metaphors
- Seize the day

Quiet Time

I never realized just how much women really crave silence until I began to conduct daylong workshops on the road. These days are a mixture of my talking and the women's working through creative exercises and filling out several worksheets. The venues vary— church sanctuaries, camps, conference halls in hotels, even a nursery greenhouse—but mandatory in the middle of each workshop is a half-hour solo "journey." This half-hour cannot replicate the Saturday beach walk, and sometimes the only sign of nature is a potted fern in a hotel hallway. But during my year alone, I came to understand that silence is an invaluable friend. When we are silent, our feelings progress naturally, our thoughts settle into order, and we can hear our dreams. Many women, however, fear silence. For them it is the twin shadow of isolation and loneliness, or it stands as a rebuke to the value they have placed on doing for others, or it beats back the walls they have erected around their pain. Too many women must be coaxed into quiet time, and so, regardless of the venue, I send my workshop attendees off to find a place, a word, a metaphor for their lives somewhere nearby in silence.

Recently, at a retreat in a church, I asked three hundred women to go quietly from the sanctuary and find a place of peace. Without a sound, they departed. Some headed for the altar and tucked in next to its freestanding table; one went to sit by the piano; still another retreated up into the choir loft. Some donned parkas and umbrellas (it was raining) and went for a walk on the grounds; some went to the Sunday school, and others to the nursery, to sit in the little chairs or on the floor of the darkened hallway. Wherever they chose to hide, no one wanted to come back after just half an hour. The women weren't ready to leave their thoughts, their spot, their new intentions, or the silence.

You don't need a magnificent beach or a grand mountain or the red rocks of Sedona to come up with a new direction for your life. For most of us, half an hour of thought-filled silence will do the job.

WHAT I FOUND AT THE BEACH

I found this gnarly piece of driftwood with a shell caught in one of its crevices. I am the shell, because I have allowed myself to get caught in the clutches of others.

I found this ancient old horseshoe crab, its shell weighted down with barnacles, unable to move itself out with the tide, and so left to die on the shore. I came to this retreat weighted down with barnacles. As I walked on after meeting that noble horseshoe crab, I began to pick off the barnacles I carry before I got stuck on the shore to die. I picked off bad voices, sad friends, the fear of failure, disregard for my body, and more. This will be an ongoing task until I am barnacle-free.

I picked up a beautiful, empty conch shell and held it to my ear to listen for the sound of the ocean, just like I used to do as a child. I had to strain to hear beyond the honking of the gulls, the howling of the wind, and the roaring of the fierce ocean. My lesson was to begin to strain to hear my own voice, to block out the others at whatever cost.

I was drawn to the seaweed—piles of green, velvety strings all tangled up with one another. At first I thought how tangled up I was, but then I focused on the seaweed itself. It is so rich and fertile. People collect seaweed and use it in their gardens. Being tangled up with such "good medicine"—good people, good ideas—will keep me rich and fertile forever. It is the dried seaweed and the broken shells that I need to steer myself around.

I found a string of toenail shells, one stuck to another, smelling terrible. Aha, I thought, if we cling to one another, the relationship begins to give off a stench. I prefer to fly free, like the gulls, wherever the wind takes me.

I looked down at the wet sand and saw hundreds of gull footprints going in every direction. I smiled, because they reminded me of what my footprints must look like right now—so much to do and pulled in so many directions. In the middle of the prints, I spotted a half-buried stone shaped like a heart. It was a reminder to take care of myself.

Body and Soul

*"When we neglect what matters most to us,
that then becomes the matter with us."*

PAULA REEVES

Getting Physical

After the long beach walk and the sharing that follows, I am usually both elated and haunted—elated by the number of women who seem to have shifted and grown from the experience, and haunted by the few who have not. I can spot the angst in this latter group as they listen to the others talk about their discoveries, and I feel their disappointment in themselves, sometimes even a sense of shame about having stood on the sidelines. These are the ones who either opted to remain behind at the inn, never got off the boat and returned after seeing the seals, or did the walk but somehow resisted the experience. For whatever reason, whether they felt out of shape, overweight, or medically indisposed, all of these women were unable to trust themselves or their bodies.

The beach walk is a test—a physical test that forces women to trust themselves in a wild, isolated, and unfamiliar place, to test their endurance, and to embark on a journey that offers no exits. It is meant to challenge their ability to open their souls to the unknown—to a limitless, uncontrollable experience, and to solitude. But most of all, it is meant to challenge their bodies.

On the beach walk, you can't help paying attention to your body. Your heart races, your pulse quickens, your legs become leaden as you work against the sand, your shoes and clothing grow heavy with sea spray, and your body chills in the wind. Why do such a trek? Because, more than anything else, this long, strenuous adventure forces a woman to affirm her emotional and physical capability. And as Joan Erikson used to say, "In order not to fail, in the end you have to be dependent on yourself and know that you can handle things."

It is always surprising to me how many women are more comfortable testing themselves emotionally, opening their hearts and minds to new perspectives, than they are addressing, let alone testing their bodies. For many women, the sheer physicality of the beach walk is too daunting and makes them doubt themselves. Yet I came to see during my year alone that I could not hope to seize my days if I left my body out of the equation. We must reacquaint ourselves with our bodies and learn to trust their capabilities in order to recognize not only their strength, but also their beauty. Spiritual enlightenment goes hand in hand with physical enlightenment. But this proposition is very scary at first, because many of us have been taught not to really know or engage their bodies.

I was no exception. I had long since avoided even looking at myself, especially when I was naked. I used to step out of the shower, grab a towel, and drape it around my middle, all the while maneuvering to keep my back to the mirror so as not to catch a glimpse of my less-than-perfect curves and bulges. I did glance in the mirror a few times before getting married, and I worked hard to rearrange what I saw through diets and exercise. Once before that I had worked hard to get in shape for a state beauty pageant in which my mother entered me. In typical fashion, I had pushed and pulled my flesh like Play-Doh into a desirable shape, mostly for men and the adoration of an audience. It never dawned on me to nourish my body for health reasons, or to honor all that it helped me do on a daily basis.

Even when I first moved to the Cape and was forced to haul wood, shovel snow, rake up dead leaves, and shuck clams as quickly as any of the other fish-market employees, I took the power of my body for granted, paying it little heed. I ate and drank whatever I wanted, shunned regular doctor visits, and let go of little indulgences such as long bubble baths and occasional massages. After all, I had run away to find myself and to feel some inner peace, not to worry about what I looked like.

I suppose you could say that from the beginning I was trained to be a "female impersonator," a term Gloria Steinem used to describe Marilyn Monroe's psyche. According to Steinem, Monroe was obsessed with trying to be who she thought others wanted her to be—with perfecting her persona rather than exploring her inner world. Her body was her canvas, but it remained utterly unconnected to her own instincts, thoughts, and desires.

So many of us women fall prey to this dangerous syndrome, viewing our bodies as something to be used to please others, to help us fit in, and perhaps, worst of all, as something to hide our authentic selves behind. "Angst about her body," says Clarissa Pinkola Estes, "robs a woman of her creative style and attention to other things. Even though the body," she explains, "protects, supports, and fires the spirit, even though it is a repository for memory and desire, most of us see it as the root of our undoing.

For sure, I was no exception as I continued to cram myself into Playtex girdles and padded bras. "Figure faults," as my mother used to refer to them, were camouflaged by clever clothes so that contours, moods, and mannerisms could all conform to a single ideal of beauty and behavior. Over time, my body meant no more to me than a projection of the persona that I was trained to present. Forget about my insides—those hidden, dark, secret places that created all manner of effluvia, where dirty things happened and dirty feelings began. In fact, I was so estranged from my inner workings that I became a hypochondriac, always in fear that my body, because it was unknown, would betray me. And so the gap widened—I lived on the outside and denied that there even was an inside, all the while eroding my ability to trust my physical strength. I skipped meals and drank dehydrated shakes to look healthy and slim. I tore off my ratty T-shirt when my husband came home from work, ran a comb through my hair, and layered on the pink lipstick, just so that I could appear cheery and pulled together.

But as Alice Miller so aptly put it: "Our intellect can be deceived; our feelings manipulated; our perceptions confused; our bodies tricked with medication; but some day this body will present its bill, for it is as incorruptible as a child who, still whole in spirit, will accept no compromises or excuses and it will not stop tormenting us until we stop evading the truth."

To Thine Own Body Be True

My body finally sounded its wake-up call when I ran a 5K New Year's Day road race. I reached the finish line huffing and puffing and dead last, but I crossed it, all because my strong legs and hearty lungs hung in and joined forces with my determined spirit. I felt both triumphant and very, very humble. Even though I hadn't trained a minute before this silly costumed race, my old body somehow endured. As I bent over to still my wobbly legs and draw in smooth, deep breaths, I was finally forced to recognize my body and begin to give it a modicum of care and attention. Joan Erikson had been cautioning me to do so for some time—"You don't looked stretched," she would say in her characteristically dry way. "It's as if you haven't gotten out of maternity!"

After the road race, I began to take her little barbs seriously. I also really took notice of how regularly she walked and how well she ate, *not* to maintain appearances, but to keep herself from getting stuck with something that was weak, injured, and uncooperative. "Our bodies are our power," she would say as if uttering a mantra. "In any case, it's the only vessel we have to help us along—a portable world—a wonder, really. You must feel confident about your body," she continued. "It really does have the capability of getting you through almost anything."

And so, when I decided to hike the Inca Trail, I drew heavily on her faith in her body and was eager for both her advice and her encouragement.

"How long before you take off?" she asked.

"Eight weeks," I answered.

"Oh, that gives us plenty of time to get you trained," she said with relief.

I had been walking regularly ever since the 5K, and Joan suggested that I build on that beginning. "After you do your morning walk, why not come here and do a half-hour on the treadmill, and then finish up with some steps."

"Steps?" I asked. She insisted that I would be able to climb any mountain if I practiced going up and down the twenty steps that led to her deck ten times with a loaded pack on my back!

"Your mind will play tricks on you, my dear, especially in those high altitudes. You want to make your muscles do for you what your mind won't. You saw how your body supported your dream of finishing the road race," she continued. "This Inca Trail adventure will be the ultimate test. You simply must go prepared."

And so the training commenced—five days a week. Each "get-acquainted session," as I called them, helped me to gain confidence in what my body would be capable of doing. Joan had long since told me to get out of my head and into my body, and her delight in my progress was infectious. "You'll see—action and motion will conspire to bring you to a new level of happiness and vision." Indeed it did. As the training continued, something I never believed could happen happened. I began to feel a convergence—ever so gradually, my body and soul were no longer separate entities. With every stretch I became more connected to muscle, tendon, limb, and organ. With fists no longer clenched, I embraced the effort, overcoming one obstacle or distance in order to reach another. As sweat poured off my forehead and I reached new aerobic levels, a passion for exercise as well as the trip began to build. My lungs were working hard, like an accordion at an endless wedding reception; muscle was replacing sagging flesh, and I was actually building a body that could help me to live into my life and seize any adventure or opportunity that came my way.

When I finally stood at the Sun Gate after four days of trekking on the Inca Trail—the climax of the hike itself—I felt physically and spiritually triumphant! My body and I had pushed through altitude, eventful weather, perilous terrain, and, on one day, fourteen hours of nonstop hiking. There was a new swagger in my step as I marched into the ancient city, walking past tourists who had come by train rather than hike. I was reborn and ready for more.

A New Perspective on High Maintenance

Several women who have come to my retreats have had similar awakenings. Joyce Ann (the woman who buried her bathroom scales on South Beach) suddenly realized the deep connection between physical and spiritual health when she was diagnosed with a blood disorder. "I wouldn't buy into the diagnosis," she told me, "because that meant giving up responsibility for my body. As soon as I stood to lose that, I realized how important it was." Joyce Ann decided to give herself a physical challenge as a way of triumphing over her body's disease, and so she set aside twelve months to train for a climb up Mount Kilimanjaro in Tanzania. This was not her first adventure; she had always been sporty and craved being out in the wilderness. Her passions had taken her to the Arctic to kayak, and to Denali National Park in Alaska for numerous adventure trips. But her preparation for Kilimanjaro was different.

Joyce Ann hired a trainer and worked out two or three times a week. She also consulted a nutritionist and a homeopathic doctor. "I decided to use the entire experience as a package to address all of my body's issues. I couldn't imagine life unless I could continue to have powerful experiences in the wild, and I never wanted to be in a place where I wanted to do something but my *body* balked. My illness helped me to see how much more I could pay attention to—not just my fitness or strength, but my entire well-being."

When she finally went on her climb, Joyce Ann made it two-thirds of the way up to the summit before her nose began to bleed, forming icicles from her nostrils. She had made a pact with the mountain to warn her when it would be time to stop. "I think this is my summit," she said to her African guide. "I have gone far enough."

"Indeed," he answered. "But I know of no other African grandmother who has gone this far."

Joyce Ann seeks out adventures, not just to reach one goal or another, but for the journey itself and the lessons each experience teaches her. "Climbing mountains or back-packing in the wilderness inevitably changes you," she says. "The person you were at the onset is not who you become when the journey is finished. That is why I am always look-ing for the next adventure."

Betsy from Philadelphia began to seek daily adventures as she watched her mother succumb to Alzheimer's.

As I saw my mother gradually disappear, I made a decision to make sure that I would live each day and not merely ex-ist. Action and energy became paramount in my daily life. Although a back injury forced me to stop playing tennis, I was quick to pick up kayaking and fly-fishing. Paddling up creeks and into marshland and then just stopping alto-gether and floating for a while gave me back the quiet time I was craving. It dawned on me that, after a childhood of playing in the woods, catching frogs, ladybugs, and worms, I had been missing all that wonder and needed it back. When a friend called and invited me to go on a trip down a river in Montana, I resisted at first, until she told me the organization running the trip was called Real Women. That changed my mind. We fished for six days on river rafts, covering sixty miles, with just two women per raft and a guide in the middle. It was a truly enlightening expe-rience. I love the way fishing takes me outdoors and keeps me connected to my childhood. I have learned to read the water, to stand for hours on end in the rain, to camp, to get

over my fear of snakes and bears, and to be alone. I feel
that I am living my days as fully as I can when I fish. I feel
healthy and happy because my body and soul are focused
on the same goal. They are poised and strong together.

More and more I am finding myself drawn to people like Joyce Ann and Betsy—women who are at home in their bodies and respectful of the deep connection between their physical and spiritual well-being, women who have achieved "physical presence." You immediately sense the empowerment such women gain from running, dancing, yoga, weight training, or walking. You can see an inner strength shining out all around them. I often joke that it is cruel to call a woman strong, because that is just another way of saying she can take on more. But these women have helped me to see strength as a matter of poise and perspective. They are strong because they have gotten the balance right—they have united body and soul.

The question then becomes, how can we stand up for our desires, feel unique and worthy of existence, and then act from there? Clearly the women who have a fire in their eyes after a road race or an adventure know better than most (or have fought to learn) what it means to truly exist. Their experience, their aliveness is palpable. They aren't simply going through the paces of living—they seem to have an eagerness about their very existence.

Nancy arrived at a weekend retreat after having just run

the Dublin Marathon. "I would never have had the guts to do anything—not even to come to this retreat—if I hadn't started running," she told me. "I was paralyzed in an unhealthy marriage, working for a miserable boss, and literally frozen in Minnesota—I thought I'd never escape."

Stuck in all areas of her life, Nancy had no place to turn except to her body—which she had fortunately always respected, but very rarely leaned upon. So she started running—first to the end of her street and back, then a little farther, then with a friend whose habit was to run two miles a day. Within three months, Nancy had lost twenty pounds and was signed up for a 5K Race for the Cure. The irony of it was that a few months later she was diagnosed with rheumatoid arthritis.

What's more, I was told that running would serve to keep the disease at bay. So now, instead of just running away from my bad marriage and job, I was running to clear my head, lift my spirit, conquer my silly fears, and save my life. Running has helped to shape who I've become—it has helped me get more in touch with my feelings and emotions. I feel the world around me and what's inside me more intensely, and as a result I live my life more passionately. It has shaped my inner being, and ultimately it has, and will, shape how I project myself to the world. I can't be restricted anymore. I think everyone needs physical activity to get in touch with themselves.

The End of Body Bashing

Like Nancy, Betsy, and Joyce Ann, I know that I am not perfect, but now that I feel my body and soul working together, I know that I'm good enough—good enough to climb a mountain, carry my grandbabies, walk five miles without hesitation, or put in a twelve-hour workday with energy left to spare. I've become a high-maintenance woman—no longer frequenting beauty parlors but, rather, the gym or a health spa, always on the lookout for my next adventure or crazy challenge.

Which brings me back to the women who stopped—those retreaters who were not yet ready to seize their day. The beach walk is meant to encourage a connection between body and soul, between physical and spiritual regeneration, that will leave the women feeling exhilarated and strong. But for some, the fear and habit of defeat are too ingrained to overcome. The good news is that, just as the life-cycle exercise can help us to see adversity as strength and possibility for growth in every situation, so a body forsaken is always recoverable. Joan Erikson always insisted, "There is autonomy and growth as we grow older, but only if we take care of our bodies. It's easy to blame the terrain or the wind for our failings and backsliding. But where the body is concerned, there is no place for self-pity. A lifetime of training is required."

Any woman considering retreat and repair should also consider training her body. As with anything else, start small—start by trusting this miraculous vessel rather than ignoring it. As I began to make friends with my body, I began to review how it had been there for me, like a faithful dog, eager for more action and affection even though I had left her out in the cold or forgotten to feed her her dinner. So— I invite you to stop your silent body-bashing by answering the following questions:

- What has your body done for you over your lifetime?

- What thankless tasks and supportive services has it supplied?

- What is your body actually capable of doing here and now?

- What body parts (bone structure, facial features, mannerisms, and the like) were inherited from distant relatives?

- What is right with your body?

- What is wrong with your body?

- What are you capable of fixing?

After answering the questions, circle all the positives. I would venture to guess that there is much more right with the vessel you inhabit than wrong. It's time to give it praise rather than your daily dose of criticism and disdain.

Here's to Self-Care

The next step is to care for your body and your soul together. Society likes to separate women's bodies from their souls, but we can defeat this dangerous attitude by revising the way we attend to ourselves.

Back in the first chapter, I quoted Clarissa Pinkola Estes on a woman's relationship to her soul. It is worth repeating here because what Estes has to say about the soul is equally important for a woman's relationship to her body:

> *Many women drive their relationship to soul as if it were a not very important instrument. Like any instrument of value, it needs shelter, cleansing, oiling, and repair. Otherwise, like a car, the relationship sludges up, causes deceleration in a woman's daily life, causes her to use up enormous energy for the simplest tasks, and finally busts down out on heartbreak ridge far away from town and telephone. Then it is a long, long walk back to home.*

All women in search of physical presence, of a life full of adventure and affirmation, must learn to shelter, cleanse, oil, and repair their bodies and souls. We've all tried to start running just to lose ten extra pounds; we've dieted before our children's weddings, or walked every day before our high-school reunion. More times than not, we've failed to achieve our goal. Why? Not because we lack the ability to lose the weight, firm up the muscle, or smooth out the wrinkles, but because our goals are all about our persona, not our whole selves. You must learn to work on your body from the inside out. Instead of identifying a physical goal, such as tightening those thighs or changing your dress size, start by identifying a dream, a passion, or a spiritual goal. Then find a physical activity to accompany it. "Nothing is worth more than working toward something of value," said Joan Erikson. I went to Machu Picchu for multiple reasons. I was envious that my kids had hiked the Inca Trail, and I wanted to know that such adventures were still within my grasp. But I also needed to refire my worn-out spirit by testing my stamina and will. Along the way, I discovered the joy of physical fitness and self-care.

SHELTER: What are some of the way you can give shelter to yourself?

CLEANSING: How can you cleanse your inner self, offer it some peace, gift it with power and blessings?

OILING: What would it mean for you to "oil" your body and soul? What would it take to feed it essentials? As with a car, what kinds of checkups and fuel does it require to keep it in tip-top shape?

REPAIR: How could you begin to repair the broken parts of your body right now—today? What types of larger repairs can you schedule for later on?

When we train our bodies to sustain our dreams, *then* we are learning to live authentically. Authentic living is not about scaling mountain peaks or winning races. It's about acknowledging and developing the God-given strength of our bodies so that we can continue to live our lives as fully as possible.

END OF CHAPTER SUMMARY

- Stop the body bashing and practice self-care
- Train your body to support your soul
- Cultivate physical presence
- Swim naked

Hot Tubbing and
Skinny Dipping

The first time I hosted a retreat on the road at a place with a hot tub, three women jumped into the hot tub after dinner stark naked. They howled with delight and the thrill of having dared to be naughty. Pretty soon the rest of us joined them. After an initial hesitation, we all just splashed around, talking and laughing with abandon. No one hid behind a towel or a swimsuit. There were fat women, skinny women, wrinkly women, and bumpy women. Some of the women had scars across their bellies, some of them had dimples in their thighs, some had flat chests, and some had breasts that sagged below their rib cages. But none of us cared what anyone else looked like. It was an amazing, liberating experience that I now try to re-create every time I get the chance. For me, naked hot-tubbing with twenty other women helps reinforce my newfound sense that my body image comes from the inside and has to do with presence, not perfection. Toni from Ohio shared her experience with me, and it captures the challenge and the reward of this experience.

> Prior to our retreat, I had heard that naked hot-tubbing was
> a distinct probability. I really wasn't sure how I felt about it.
> I have always been conscious of my body. I am in fairly
> good shape. I practice yoga, I do some weight training, and
> I jog. But I also really like licorice, wine, cookies, and ice
> cream. I have pockets of cellulite, all of which seem to be on

my left hip. The cellulite is OK—after all, I am forty-nine—but the lopsidedness makes me fret. I always wished my legs were longer and my breasts bigger. Sags and scars accompany most parts of my anatomy. Sometimes I am proud of these marks—like the scar on my belly and the little bulge that sags beneath it—the permanent, visible reminder of my two C-sections. Other marks have less meaning and just seem like flaws. I've spent most of my lifetime thinking I could be thinner, my stomach flatter, my thighs more toned, if only I worked at it harder. So what was I going to do on the retreat?

Sure enough, Joan encouraged us all to leave our fears back in our rooms with our clothes and join her in the hot tub. I checked myself out in the mirror before making up my mind. But as I did, I heard all of these other women running and laughing past my window. I am not perfect and I never will be, but I came on the retreat to escape the dictatorship of my fears and insecurities. So I took off my jeans and threw on my robe.

The thing about hot tubs is that there is no way to quickly get in with any amount of grace or ease. There were already ten people in the water when I arrived, but I was the only one still in a robe. I took the plunge and, along with the heat, I felt infused with bravery and confidence. When the next person arrived and stood above us on the edge, trying to decide what to do next, my instinct was to look only at her face and specifically her eyes as a way to protect *her modesty. But I found that her eyes were full of her emotion and her personality. Instead of avoiding intimacy, I was actually looking right at it. As soon as her eyes smiled at me, I realized her body, and my body, were inconsequential.*

For sure, I had a sense of shapes all around me. But really I was more conscious of a feeling of fullness and soft edges and most of all of history. The idea came to me that there is a sacred quality to a woman's body, a body that was designed to comfort, to nest, to hold, and to uphold. What incredible beauty I was surrounded by. My own body was validated by this experience. I felt pride in my physical self and laughed at what I had perceived to be flaws. My body holds my history and it holds my experience. I am real and my body is real. Most important, beauty isn't found in hips or tummies but, rather, in our spirit, our mind, and our soul.

Not all women can take the risk Toni took, but the idea of skinny-dipping in the hot tub inspires them to think more about finding their own rituals to honor their bodies. During a recent California retreat, when the inevitable naked hot-tub idea began to make its way through the group of attendees, unbeknownst to me one woman was appalled—appalled that it seemed as if I had insisted that if you didn't strip you couldn't be part of the experience. She confessed to me at the retreat's end that she had many body issues, had fought both bulimia and anorexia for years, was now pleasantly plump, and couldn't bear disrobing in front of others. Even though we all seemed nonjudgmental, her history told her otherwise. She harbored some anger toward me and disappointment in herself. But as the weekend progressed, she was smart enough to know this was *her* problem and it should be addressed. Her solution? To have her own private hot-tub experience—to slip into the pool when no one else was around and to begin once again to know the joy of her body.

Getting naked seems to have become a rite of passage for those who finally want to come to terms with and accept the bodies that they were given. Most mornings during the Cape Cod weekends, the women get their coffee and huddle on a nearby beach to watch the sun come up. On one such weekend, I found an unusually large number of women anxious for the orange ball to pop up from beyond the horizon, but also clearly anxious for something else. As the sun rose and the fishing boats chugged by for a day at sea, one after another of the women ceremoniously stripped and ran for the water! In minutes there were a dozen or more women splashing about, utterly delighted that they had dared themselves to swim with the seals and actually followed through on their plan.

On other weekends, I am likely to find one or more women floating at the tip of South Beach, again swimming with the seals, and pleased with themselves for braving the chilly water, stripping in front of others, and finally feeling the rush that comes whenever one swims in the nude—no cloth or constraint between body and water. It is a freeing experience, a deviation from the rules, totally unconventional, and for the most part outrageous. I suppose that's why not a weekend goes by without one woman or another pushing the envelope—delighting in herself and her body no matter what others might think.

Joan Erikson believed that the way to enjoy life was to be outdoors, with the elements, and the fewer clothes on the better. I have adopted her mantra now that I have watched so many women feel determined and delighted by the chance finally to revel in the sensuous and enjoy their bodies.

TRAINING BODY AND SOUL

The most important consideration when you commit yourself to the repair of your body is to know what is in it for your soul. The weekend women have found many ways to build bodies that can support their dreams. Here are some of their suggestions:

Participate in Race for the Cure on Mother's Day

Learn to sail, kayak, fly-fish, skydive

Volunteer to coach a local youth sport team

Bike to errands

Walk to and from work

Take an overnight hike up a mountain

Build with Habitat for Humanity

Sign up for a walking tour through Napa Valley with friends

Plan and prepare for an overnight bike trip with your grandchildren

Become a certified Pilates instructor

Swim the 100 IM with your daughter

Regroup by Finding Balance and Boundaries

Surrender Everyone Else's Expectations

> *"When one leaves certain social situations,*
> *moves into temporary loneliness, and then finds a*
> *few jewels, everything changes."*
>
> JOSEPH CAMPBELL

Waking Up

By Sunday morning, a mild euphoria fills the inn. The women's faces shine with what C. S. Lewis describes as "felt satisfaction: a quiet joy mixed with a sense of gratefulness." By taking time away, and by daring to put a relationship with themselves first, all of the women have begun to experience a budding sense of sureness. They know their time has come, that they are on a rising swell, no longer stuck like a ship on life's sandy shoals.

On this particular morning, I follow several women who are meandering down to the beach to watch the sunrise.

With a steaming cup of coffee in hand, I stay a few steps behind so as not to intrude, conscious that they have just this one day of solitude left. I am pleasantly struck by their body language. This is definitely not the same group of fractured, fearful women who sat in a circle yesterday, or the day before, and silently challenged me to show them the way out of their confusion. I can tell just by watching their shoulders relax and their legs bounce that these women are enormously content. They seem to have come to terms with the fact that they are right where they should be—that this moment is enough—that, as is said in Ecclesiastes, "To every thing there is a season." There is a time to mother, a time to love, a time to relate, a time to withdraw, a time to care for others, and a time to care for self.

I know from previous retreats that the women who come to the beach on this last day feel worthy of a meaningful future. They see now that the roles they spent a lifetime perfecting have diminished or run their course altogether, and they understand the sentiment of Carl Jung: "To hold on to anything ruins it."

During a mere thirty-six hours, most of the women have developed a full-blown case of self-determination, and now feel comfortable accepting the idea of change. The weekend has gone through more than one full tide cycle, and so have these women. They've grown accustomed to the rhythm of ebb and flow; they have felt the shorelines of their lives begin to soften and re-form; and they have welcomed the waves of truth and insight that have washed over them.

Way back on Friday, they were hardly able to articulate why they needed to retreat. Some suggested that they were "called"; others said they followed a hunch or gave in to a whim; some admitted to simply accepting a friend's blind invitation. Regardless of what first spurred them on, they all came because at some level they trusted their instincts. As the weekend has unfolded and their perspectives have shifted, they are growing to understand the importance of their actions—something that in the beginning seemed a bit luxurious, indulgent, or random is now seen as a necessary response to a valid need. Alone, under the big sky, with few constraints, insufficiencies have been accepted, mistakes measured, bad choices analyzed, needs acknowledged, and desires given a stronger voice. Most significantly, these women have set themselves free of other people's stories, of caution and prudence, of sadness and wrongdoing. Adventures always seem to become wellsprings for the human spirit, and the hallmark of these retreats is adventure.

Ellen wrote in her journal that on Sunday morning she simply woke up.

I can only explain it as something more than an everyday regaining of consciousness—I had transcended the mundane. Overnight it became clear what I had to do. In fact, I felt actually silly that I hadn't been able to see my future this clearly before. For so long, I had felt that something was missing. When I woke up on Sunday, that weight had lifted and was replaced with an urge to take control and move on. I was happy because I knew what I wanted to do, and I knew that I was strong enough to do it. The metaphor of the molting lobster finally made sense. Just like a lobster, I had been hiding out in order to grow a sturdy shell. Deep down I always knew that I wanted to stop being just what everyone wanted me to be; now I also knew that I could make whatever changes I had to, because I was happy inside my own shell.

The poet Antonio Machado says, "Between living and dreaming there is something more important—waking up." This waking up is an intense state of awareness, which in turn creates an unabashed euphoria—the miracle that occurs when we step away from ordinary life and permit the subconscious to meet the conscious. Ellen and all the other retreaters have learned at last to listen to themselves—to become masters of their own destinies, finally able to embrace their very essential inner guides.

Love Letters from the Sand

With the confluence of so many emotions, it would be all too easy for the women to let Sunday morning slip through their fingers. But it is important that they hold on to this abundant bliss and design a life that keeps them away from the straight lines once and for all.

For these reasons, after sunrise, I pass out paper and pens so that each woman can write a letter to herself—as if to her best friend—describing her retreat and answering such questions as: When and where did you begin to feel contentment? Did you first feel peace on the beach or when you arrived at the inn? Were you alone or with the group, in the hot tub or just waking up in the morning? Perhaps you felt peace the minute you left home, boarded the airplane, or got in your car and turned up the radio. Maybe it was when you were being served dinner, or saw the fresh flowers in your room, or lived in the same sweatpants the whole time. "However peace came to you," I say, "record it in your letter to yourself. Put the letter in an envelope, address and seal it. In a month or so, I will send you your thoughts."

Many women have told me that they hold on to these letters as a reminder of how good it feels to live for themselves. Aly and Francine keep their letters readily accessible so as never to forget or regress.

Dear Aly:

I am on the most amazing journey. Right now I am sitting in the sand on a beach on Cape Cod. The sun is just beginning to peep up over the ocean. I am surrounded by thirty-three other women who I did not know two days ago, and now feel as if I have known forever. They have become my sisters. I feel so comforted by them and so relaxed. You know what a big decision it was for me to attend this weekend. The moment I finished the last page of the book A Year by the Sea, I knew I had to come here. But I have never traveled so far, and I didn't know if Ralph would approve or support me. As I made my arrangements, I felt so much excitement, but doubt still haunted me. I had just quit my job of seventeen years, and I had promised myself that I would greet this crossroads of my life by integrating courage and strength so that I could move forward. But I did not feel very much of either.

Even that first evening, when we all gathered and shared parts of our stories, I did not feel strong or capable. In fact, I wanted to go home. I do not like being in groups of people and I have never been comfortable talking about myself. I can't even join an aerobics class, but would prefer to walk alone. Joan has pushed us to be alone, but she has also drawn us out into a place in this group. I first started to relax when I actually had to share my story. It was so hard to talk about my relationship with Ralph and my decision to leave my job because of his health. I cried a lot, but so did a few other women. So many of them feel the same confusion about their relationships and choices. When we went to dinner that night, I was happy and surrounded by friends who understand me.

The next day we did a solo walk. For the first time, walking alone was not in reaction and out of fear, but because I knew I could leave a group and they would still be there. I now feel strong and courageous because I feel supported. When I come home, you must help me to find a group of women with whom I can share my days and my thoughts. I am not alone.

Dear Francine:

I must share with you an experience I just had here on Cape Cod with Joan Anderson. I woke up this morning with nothing to do and nowhere to go. I threw on the same shorts I wore yesterday, and for once, I did not blow-dry my hair. Yesterday was so magical because I went where I pleased and said no to others. When Joan dropped us off on the beach, I did not follow her advice and find a place for myself. I ran for a mile beside the ocean. And then I crossed over the dunes and waded in the smooth water of the bay. When I reached the lighthouse, I turned left, away from the inn, and went into town for a cup of tea by myself. When I got back, I loved sharing my experience with the other women, but I loved most that I said "No" first. I am going to say that a lot more, because it makes me happy.

The call of the wild urges freedom over fear, and after any time away in natural surroundings, we go from being careful and appropriate to daring and abandoned. Out of your very breakdown, you will experience myriad breakthroughs. These moments, lessons, and metaphors are fleeting, but they are worth recording and remembering. That is why it is important to catch your thoughts on paper—to journal and then to take the time to write a letter to yourself.

In your letter:

- Explain what made you go away—what led you to begin searching—and where are you in your journey.

- Describe your feelings—how did you feel before you got away, and what sources of contentment did you find while away?

- Most important, try to articulate what it is that you need or want to hold on to when you return to normal life. Pay special attention to any feelings or desires that may have surfaced as you worked through the earlier exercises. Identify what you want to hold on to and what you can do to live up to your intentions.

When you are done, reread what you have written. Highlight the "aha" moments, prominent desires, intentions, and needs, all of which will help you form resolutions. This may not be New Year's Eve, but it is the beginning of a new era for you. Past retreaters have recorded in their letters the resolve to be true to self; to make no more compromises; to insist on reciprocity; to make solitude a good friend; to know that today will come and go, so live it fully; to make room for time out; and to slow down and live more deliberately.

Now seal your letter and tuck it away for at least one

month, maybe two. You may want to mail it to a friend and have her mail it back to you. It is very important to revisit your thoughts and feelings. Just as looking at old photographs allowed you to see your sturdy roots, receiving this letter will help you remember that fulfillment is within your grasp. It will bring you back to your unfinished journey and alert you to the ways in which you may have too quickly resumed business as usual.

Performing a Balancing Act

Now for the concrete work of regrouping. The only real way we can hope to protect our feelings of euphoria is to devise a way to maintain balance and create some boundaries.

"For it is surely a lifetime work, this learning to be a woman," said May Sarton, and I repeat her line in almost every appearance I make, if for no other reason than to remind women that there are no easy, one-step answers. We will race forward and fall backward. The important thing is to have a plan and keep it going.

I know that, when I am leading a weekend retreat or standing behind a podium talking, it must strike many women that I have it all together, that I have done my work, changed my life, and now live happily, enjoying all of my unfinished dreams and desires. To the contrary. Yes, I have worked hard to change the direction and tone of my life, but with each new book come new tasks and busy days filled with more challenges. Like anyone else, I forget to breathe or walk or make time to feel content. I continually have to remind myself that indeed I have sturdy roots, strong desires, and the will to stretch toward my dreams. I have to check in with myself regularly, and I always have maintenance work to do.

Recently I was overbooked and undernourished. It was winter, my husband was recuperating from hip surgery, my mother had fallen and injured herself on the ice, and I was expected in Chicago to help with the birth of a new grandbaby. Needless to say, I was frantic. Did I want to go or stay? My husband hates being confined, and my mother cannot go a day without dropping in for a visit. What would they do without me? If I went, how many meals should I make and freeze? Who could I line up to check in on my husband and mother? What would they do if a heavy snowstorm came and we once again lost electricity? Did my husband know where the phone number was for the boy who shovels my mother's driveway? Yet, if I stayed, who would help my son and daughter-in-law navigate the chaos of bringing a new baby home? Who would take care of two-year-old Grady and soothe his adjustment to a new sibling? Where could I order meals for their freezer? What kind of mother or grandmother would I be if I wasn't there?

Each possibility seemed exhausting. I couldn't stop the

worrying and caretaking. I missed a work deadline and canceled lunch with a friend. The more I worried, the more I found myself getting caught up in everyone else's needs and plans. I was more concerned about helping my husband, my mother, my son, my daughter-in-law, and, yes, even my two-year-old grandson, than I was about figuring out what I needed or wanted. What would work for me right now? Where did I want to be?

I had to laugh at the way I had slipped back into the knot of everyone else's perceived expectations. I was completely beside myself, feeling stressed, compromising my own work, and skipping bits of pleasure, all so that I could figure out how to keep everyone else's life going. What would the women who came to my retreats think of me now? Couldn't I follow my own advice?

It was on the airplane flying to Chicago some days later that I caught my confusion and remembered the balance wheel. So many of the exercises in this book came out of my need to reinvent myself during my year by the sea, or from the needs of the women on the weekends. The balance-wheel exercise was invented when, after the Saturday beach walk, a woman brought back a large stone that was exactly half white and half black. "This rock is me," she exclaimed, holding it up for all to see. We stared at her and wondered how she was going to explain this clue. "I used to give all of me away to everyone else," she said. "No longer. From here on in, I will divide my life evenly into two parts.

This part," she said pointing to the white side, "will be just for me; the black section will be left for others."

Her explanation made everyone sit up and take notice. It was such a simple, graphic illustration of balance and boundaries. So I drew a large circle on the easel, and divided it in half. Then I divided each half into four parts. The self side included body, mind, spirit, and relationship. The other side included friends, family, work, and other. Together the women and I filled in the sections with everything we could

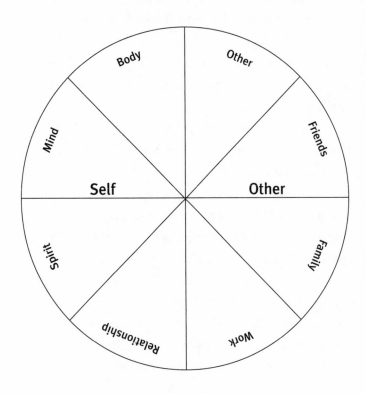

think of that was readily available and could be a way for us to take care of ourselves in each category. For *body* they came up with suggestions such as: diet, massage, exercise, sex, or walking. For *mind* they proposed: reading, therapy, journaling, attending lectures, going to museums, and sleep. For *spirit* they suggested: church, daily quiet time, meditation, yoga, getting out into nature. For *relationship* they came up with: talking each evening, find a hobby to share, exercising together, and listening. Oftentimes, the suggestions for each category overlap. Sex, for instance, has been written under body, spirit, and relationship. Exercise, quiet time, therapy, and dancing all work for any number of categories.

This same pattern surfaced when we brainstormed about the side reserved for others. For *friends* the women suggested: share a daily walk, dance, go to a museum, have lunch. For *family* they suggested: take a trip, have an adventure, look at old photographs, and plan a game night. For *work* they suggested: clean your working space, make daily lists, or take a day off.

Now I hand out sectioned circles to the women at all of my retreats. We talk about the eight categories and brainstorm together about possible activities and ideas. Each woman writes down the ideas that work for her and fills in her own full circle. She decides for herself what she needs to do to nourish her mind, her body, her career, and her family. When everyone has a full circle, I talk about how to use this wheel to achieve a sense of balance in our lives at home.

"Your goal," I explain, "is to realize one suggestion from the self categories every week. In other words, each week, make sure that you do something for your mind, your body, your spirit, and your relationship. The other side always takes care of itself. Soon your life will appear to have some semblance of balance. It will become second nature to stop and shift your focus from your mind to your friends, from your body to your family. When we feed all parts of our lives equally, then we feel whole and well nourished. We are able to give and to receive—to make each moment a chance for true reciprocity."

So, on that flight to Chicago, I had only to think about how I would take care of myself while also taking care of others. For my body I could go to a neighborhood Curves when the grandchildren were napping; I could also walk to the grocery store and do all the other necessary errands on foot. I resolved to curl up with my daughter-in-law's wonderful magazines in the evening when my son and his wife are bonding with the baby. Simply observing the blessings that an infant brings would revive my spirit, but I would also stop into the local Catholic church and take time to praise the miracle of what has occurred. There would be plenty of time for relationship—I would have to get down on the floor and play with my two-year-old grandson, and relate to my son and daughter-in-law as I helped them to cope with the additional challenges that come with a burgeoning family.

The act of simply writing down or thinking out my own prescription for my body, mind, and spirit kept me steadfast and true to the tasks at hand, enabled me to focus on the gifts I had waiting for me, and, more important, helped me to draw a boundary around my involvement. This is what results from being a scholar of self and soul. What's more, in the process of surrendering everyone else's expectations and remaining true to your own needs, you will become your very own personal coach. "It's all about taking a stand when it really matters," said Joan Erikson, "and then living up to what you've gotten hold of and not letting it melt."

I am always struck when my runner son comes to visit. Regardless of what activities we have planned, he finds the time to schedule in a run. I, on the other hand, have been known to toss my intentions to the wind in deference to the schedule of others. I do the same thing when I try to diet. I find it all too easy to cheat on my program in order to feel more a part of the group or the day, but then, of course, I lose my momentum. My son knows how to be his own coach. He is always in training for one race or another. He has on-going goals that force him to stay the course. He keeps a log-book of his training, diet, and exercise and reserves a separate calendar to chart his progress against his goals, all the while holding to his job and family responsibilities.

Use your annotated balance wheel to help you stay on track. Let it be a touchstone you revisit whenever you need to be bolstered or reminded of your goals. This is how past retreaters coach themselves through the tough times they encounter back home.

So it comes down to these questions: How much time are you spending on others and how much on yourself? Have you nourished your mind recently? Have you checked in with your body? Just as my son plans each morning when he is going to run, I, too, now pencil in time for me upon awakening. And the reward? I feel fulfilled and no longer frustrated that I gave too much of myself away.

We women have made surrendering to the wishes of others an art form. Now we need to make the impulse of surrender work for us. It is no longer about giving over and resigning in favor of another's needs. Now it is about surrendering our instinct to attend to their requests, surrendering the "shoulds," the ideals, and taking up our own needs and desires. It is about surrendering to ourselves. Then and only then will we become the women we never intended to be. Hurray! As Jean Shinoda Bolen says, "Harmony happens when behavior and belief come together—when we are living our highest truth."

END OF CHAPTER SUMMARY

- Let go of everyone else's expectations
- Aim for balance by feeding all parts of your life equally
- Become your own personal coach
- Establish clear boundaries
- Coupon for body, mind, spirit, and soul (see page 168)
- Know what to keep and what to dump

What to Keep and
What to Dump

Joan Erikson and I spent many an afternoon discussing what was truly important to each of us and what was not. She had an entire lifetime to look back on, and it seemed so easy for her to know what was superfluous and what wasn't. It is important, as we begin to seize our very individual lives back, that we know what we like and what we don't, what we need and what we can do without. If we don't understand our desires, passions, and feelings, how can we champion them? All of us women have been constrained by the roles, feelings, behaviors, and needs we have been told we *should* follow. At least half of the reason so many of us don't know what we want or feel is that we have never dared to ask the questions. Joan Erikson was not conflicted about what was good for her and what made her life pleasant and livable. One of the ways she became so clear was working on a running list of what to keep and what to dump. She periodically reviewed the list, adding here or there, and making sure that whatever could go had in fact been dumped.

Here are some of the things she would hold on to: secrets, stubbornness, independence, memories, divorce, journaling, play, ecstasy, new experiences, adventure.

Here are some of the things she would readily get rid of: regrets, judgment, tight clothes, clutter, nylon stockings.

As you learn how to become your own personal coach, try working on a list of what to keep and what to dump. Add to the list whenever something, or someone, sparks a reaction. By recording your responses, you will be able to perceive any patterns. Do you consistently want to decline a certain friend's invitations to dinner? Well, maybe it is time to do so. Next time she calls, just say no. Do you feel better every time you wear your new blue sweater? Well, go buy another one, or something else in that color.

Getting the balance right and giving to yourself is as simple as attending to your own moods and reactions as sensitively as you do to the moods and reactions of your loved ones.

COUPONING

In order to make ourselves whole, we must make time for our souls, spirits, bodies, and minds.

Make yourself a set of coupons. Label them *soul, spirit, body, mind.*

What are some of the things you could do each week that would enliven your soul, spirit, body, and mind? Write one answer on each coupon.

The weekend women have come up with these ideas:

Soul: Meditation, yoga, beach walk, attending a concert, an art museum, a church

Spirit: Play, sing, dance, have sex, pray, hold a baby, be sensual, have an adventure, go away for the day

Body: exercise, belly-dance, sleep in, take a nap, facial, massage, go to a spa, swim, bike, run

Mind: take a course, attend a lecture, read, write, journal, communicate, form a book club

Keep the coupons handy and attempt to use one in each category once a week. If you fail to cash in on any one of the four, you will need to double up on enriching that part of your life during the next week.

Gradually, you will get used to pleasing yourself.

GIVE AND TAKE QUESTIONNAIRE

"If it is a woman's nature to nurture,
then she must nourish herself."

Anne Morrow Lindbergh

1. Answer the following questions:

   How long have you been in service to others?

   How many roles do you play or have you played?

2. Record for one day how many times you are asked to:

   Give away time

   Give of your energy

   Give of your ideas

   Give sympathy or emotional support

   Listen and respond

3. Now list the number of times during the same day when someone else:

   Offered you help

   Did something for you spontaneously and without being asked

   Brought you nourishment

   Listened and responded

Gave you sympathy or emotional support

Anticipated a need

Are you giving more than you are receiving? If so, you must strive to reverse the situation. You cannot make other people give to you, but you can make sure that you spend as much time on yourself as you do on other people.

....

Regenerate by Embracing Your Second Journey

Gather Your Strengths and Sponsor Yourself

> "We human beings are in search of meaning—in search
> of ourselves. Very little of what we already are will bring
> us deeper meaning and happiness. We are born for
> meaning, not pleasure—unless it is pleasure steeped in
> meaning. We are born to overcome ourselves.
> We are searchers."

JACOB NEEDLEMAN

Embark on Your Second Journey

Suddenly it is our last afternoon together. Although still open-faced and fresh, the women are anxious about the future—not a far-down-the-road future, but the future that waits for them following the conclusion of the retreat. They have confronted everything about themselves—the shape of their faces, their family lineage, the limitations of their upbringing, their supposed lack of talent, the restrictions put on their imaginations, their flawed bodies or personalities, the choices that have locked them in, the responsibilities they carry—and they are eager to get on with their unfinished lives. Whatever disdain they may have had about any imperfection or poor choice has been turned inside out and is now seen as rich and fertile raw material with which to work. But they all know that significant challenges still await them.

"The work you've been doing up until now," I say to the women, "has unknowingly set you on a new course, and I would guess that for most of you there will be no turning back. You came on this weekend because you were at a crossroads, right? And now, with fresh insight and your intuition revived, you are beginning what is called a *second journey.*" They look at me with quizzical expressions.

"This little-known journey was brought to my attention some years ago when I picked up Father Gerald O'Collins' book *Second Journey.* In it he describes precisely what I was seeking when I ran away and what I'm guessing you all are looking for as well. According to O'Collins, second journeys commence when the power of youth is gone, when the dreams of earlier years start to seem shallow and pointless, when anxiety and self-doubt rise to the surface, and when the possibility of failure presents itself. As we've all experienced, the turmoil begins when the 'program' ends—when the predictable jobs have been completed, when you find yourself saying, Now what? In a culture that would just as soon send middle-aged people off to gated communities and put old people to bed, many of us are hard-pressed to find an original, exciting, vital way.

"This is when the idea of the second journey enters. It is an unpredictable path fraught with risk and unknowns, but if you dare to look at what's become of your life, it is an un-avoidable time. Second journeys typically begin when a rush of changes precipitates a crisis of feelings—changes such as betrayal, an unexpected loss of income or employment, a bad diagnosis, the death of a loved one. In short, you are stopped dead in your tracks. When you come to your senses, you see that you simply must stop—get away from the daily grind and the people around you, to deviate from the tried and true and to take an outer journey.

"This is precisely what you have done by coming on this weekend retreat. While you've been away, your values and goals have shifted. You've begun to see that you are stand-ing at a crossroads and that you alone must decide the next move. In the words of Robert Frost: 'Two roads diverged in a wood, and I—I took the one less traveled by.' Second jour-neys entail lots of struggles, not the least of which is to fig-ure out which new path to take. But what sets these important journeys apart is that they are all about moving forward in a meaningful way.

"On one of my forays to a nearby pond, I came across a

family of frogs hopping about the marsh and the shore. Their bulging eyes, pulsating tummies, and funny, throaty sounds mesmerized me. But the 'aha' moment came when I saw that they never once hopped backward. I learned later that frogs never do—they only hop forward. What a great symbol for all of us woman in transition—onward, forward, and don't even think of going backward!

"I have been fascinated with looking forward since my first meeting with Joan Erikson on the jetty. When she suggested walking out to the very tip, I was surprised, because it was such a foggy, stormy day, and the rough sea was tumbling over the rocks. She noticed my hesitation and quickly said, 'I've left a lot of baggage back on shore, dear. I tend not to look back or linger in the past. I am so much more interested in what's ahead.'

"Your time away this weekend marks the beginning of a second journey that you will continue when you return home. You will keep moving forward, because you have learned what it feels like to be at home in your own skin—to be alone and love it, to be free. Remember, if Momma ain't happy, than no one is happy. Besides, there's really no alternative anymore, is there? All of you will return to ringing phones, needy loved ones, curious friends, and demanding jobs, but business as usual is no longer an option. Your path now is filled with new intentions. It is time to gather your strengths and sponsor yourself."

A Second-Journey Poster Child

The idea of a second journey can be overwhelming for many women, because it highlights the fact that "unfinished" sounds as if there is hardly a destination in sight. Fortunately, you have the stories of past retreaters who have actually taken the turns in their roads, embraced new adventures, and reinvented themselves. Ellen, a retreater from whom you've already heard, calls herself the poster child for the second journey.

Before coming on the weekend, everything in my life had shifted. My older son went to college; my other son got his driver's license and simply flew the coop; my husband, who had a prescription-drug dependency, got clean; the house we had been building for years was finally finished, and with it the daily barrage of questions from workmen; and on top of it all, it was no longer necessary for me to work for my husband so that I could have flexible hours for the family—no one needed me around as much, and our finances had taken an upward turn. In short, I suddenly found myself with no purpose whatsoever!

The first thing I did was get onto my treadmill, spend more time outside, watch Seinfeld *reruns, and pet the dog. Then I started going to Al-Anon meetings to better under-*

stand my husband's new behavior. Lo and behold, I came to see how terribly codependent I was. That realization led me to such things as Kabala meetings (Jewish mysticism), taking a photography course, and eventually putting together a group of like-minded empty-nesters. Someone in that group gave me An Unfinished Marriage and A Year by the Sea. I read both books and then attended a weekend, which turned out to be enormously empowering. For the first time I was able to step beyond my own dependency on others; I came to see myself as an individual, not somebody's something. Still I wasn't sure how to move forward.

Meanwhile, my husband had embraced a whole new world that I did not fit into comfortably. It soon became obvious that we were two struggling souls going in very different directions. I had a lot of grieving to do over the failing marriage, and I had a very hard time letting go. Then, one day, I started questioning why I was in the grocery store buying cleaning supplies for the empty house! No one really lived there. The kids had detached. My husband had detached. Even I had detached! I took everything out of the cart, put it back on the shelves, and walked out of the store empty-handed. I felt like I was in a movie, and I could hear all the women in the theater cheering. Just like that I began to create my own life.

From that moment on I felt again the freedom I had experienced on the weekend. What's more, the longer I stood on my own, the more I put myself first. I continued to seek direction through healers and therapy, and I began to truly love the exploration. For one thing, I began to understand that you can never know when, where, or if the journey will end. The stumbling, falling, and rethinking are all part of the task at hand. On a more personal note, I learned in therapy that I had been mirroring my rational, rarely humorous, and always under-control mother all of these years. I had long ago detached from my wild, silly, passionate self. I needed to feel passionate again, and I needed to have my own dreams, not just share my husband's. So, when I heard about a yearlong program that would lead me into counseling work, I applied. I had begun to feel a real pull toward the healing field, and I grabbed the confidence I needed to walk through the first open door that I saw.

"The transitions of life's second half offer a special kind of opportunity to break with social conditioning and do something new and different," says William Bridges in his book *Transitions: Making Sense of Life's Changes.* That is just what Ellen did. She recognized her personal gifts and passions and decided to begin to use them. Her real self was no longer obscured by what she was supposed to be. She had come of age and found what was meant for her.

A Good Life Is the Best Revenge

Ellen's story has inspired many women. After all, "Living well is the best revenge," writer George Herbert said. Once you've stepped off the track and begun to reclaim control of your life, the next step is to fashion a good life for yourself. Just as Ellen learned, we can only become something new by ceasing to be something old. The goal is for your mid-life crisis to turn into a mid-life discovery. All you must do is follow the advice of theologian Frederick Buechner and continue to "listen to your life for its fathomless mystery."

Ellen is one example of someone who reacted to all the changes thrust upon her and as a result allowed her own dreams for the future to unfold. Nicole, on the other hand, was also caught up in a whirl of changes, but she repressed her individual wants and desires in an effort to minimize the impact of her mid-life crisis. Her children had left home, her husband had changed jobs, and her father had become increasingly dependent, but Nicole did everything she could to keep her feelings under wraps so as not to rock the boat. "I was angry as hell," this mild-mannered bookstore-owner wrote to me after her retreat, "but I was frozen as well."

The way I had lived my life for thirty years had been to repress just about every emotion so as not to make waves.

Then I came upon your book. I was captured by the cover and went off to the back room in the bookstore to read it. Your feelings were my feelings. I don't usually mark up books, but I couldn't help myself. I underlined everything! There was no question I had to go on a weekend. While on Cape Cod, the book came to life for me—that retreat and meeting the other women, all of us with the very same feelings, changed my attitude. I realized for the very first time that I had never taken a whole weekend for me. How pitiful is that? What the hell's the matter with me? I wondered. What kind of idiot are you, Nicole, that you haven't done anything like this before?

When I went back to California, I slipped right back into my old habit of ignoring the idea of change and conflict. I felt so good after the retreat, and I thought that could be enough. But when the euphoria began to wear off, I went crazy. Everything that had been bottled up in me came spilling out. My poor husband had no idea what was happening as my mild-mannered personality turned sharp and opinionated. Even so, he surely listened and took notice. The intention I declared at the retreat was honesty. I knew that, in order to fully live my life, I had to start being less secretive with myself and everyone else around me. So, when I started to feel myself spiral back into my old angst, I just let it all pour out of me. Everything I had thought and felt for years, I forced myself to lay on the table. I talked about my longings, my desire to someday live where there were seasons, that I wanted to go back to Cape Cod, that I wanted to do anything but continue living the way I had been.

When I started sharing all of my feelings, I felt very scared. I was so used to holding everything in and keeping myself quiet. But the more I put out there, the more I felt the strength and euphoria come back. Best of all, my husband surprised us both and made it easy.

He got it—at least somewhat. We had plans to gut the kitchen that summer, but when I stopped talking, he looked at me and said: "Do you really want to gut the kitchen, or do you want to take a road trip around the country?" We took the road trip—I suppose you could call it our outer journey. I needed to stretch myself and learn to be more honest, but if we were going to escape the stagnancy our life had acquired, we had to work together to get our relationship on a much more even keel. Aside from a few glitches at the beginning, it turned out to be a wonderful turnaround time for both of us. We laughed and talked, and shared our thoughts on everything and every place we visited. In the end, we bought a B & B in Woodstock, Vermont, and moved out east. We spent the first thirty years of our marriage making our life together miserable because we were so careful and closed and conventional. We've dedicated the next thirty years to making our life great.

We Are Our Choices

Both Ellen and Nicole needed to feel a passion again and learn how to walk toward their dreams. They instinctively realized that "to have a sense of meaning (or a sense of self) is to not have the answers," as Carl Jung said, "but to be aware that one has been addressed or called, as living, after all, is a response!"

Still, not every retreater heeds her inner voice or knows how to respond so quickly. It took me several years after the year I spent alone by the sea, to really see how my values and needs had shifted, and then there was the struggle to figure out which path I should follow. Denise is an example of one woman working with such a dilemma. You may remember, she spent six weeks here on Cape Cod. When she returned home, she was still questioning, among many things, whether or not to stay married. Having never had children, she didn't have to consider anyone but herself. Even so, she was stumped. I suggested that she write down the things she was passionate about. Her list was eclectic but concrete, and it included such things as:

Photography—human interest

HIV/AIDS Africa

Women's studies/gender issues/sexuality

Writing

Cape Cod

One afternoon she went to a meeting at her old university to talk about working toward a master's degree in women's studies—the safest and securest item on her list. When she got into the elevator, there was a lone flyer taped to the back wall announcing an informational session on working with families affected by HIV/AIDS in Kenya. "That flyer called to me," she told me recently.

I skipped the original meeting and followed my instincts. By the end of the day, I had signed up, written a check, and started to pack. I didn't think twice about it—I didn't even ask my husband. I knew that this move would lead to other moves. As soon as I made the decision, I knew I had taken an important first step.

For the first time, I feel that I am on my way—my own way. I am able to trust the journey, and I am not even anxious about reaching any set goal or seeing the shape of my future. Of course I'll be taking a camera along with me. Maybe a book will come out of this adventure!

Denise, like Ellen and Nicole, has learned to listen to her heart and make choices for herself, not waiting for the one perfect, sensible choice to rise to the surface. The result is that she feels delighted rather than trapped. "We are our choices," said Jean-Paul Sartre. Indeed, every new step we take, each new opportunity that we dare to seize, repays us with a more exciting life and increased confidence in our very being.

Never-Ending Crossroads — Multiple Choices

Just inside my front door, I have a wall of crosses that I have collected over the years. Although I consider myself to be spiritual, these crosses are not a religious shrine—rather, they are a constant reminder of the many crossroads I have encountered and the many choices that I have at any time. My cross wall invites me to always look ahead, stay open, and welcome whatever lies around the bend. One way to keep yourself moving forward into your second journey is to look at just how many choices you actually have.

At the weekends and the workshops I conduct on the road, I hand out sheets of blank crosses such as on page 187. At the center of the cross, put down a category, or a specific issue, that you are dealing with right now. Are you trying to decide whether to change jobs? Or leave a relationship? Or perhaps you are unhappy and feeling blocked by your body or your financial situation. Whatever it is that is stopping you, write it down in the center of the cross.

Now take some time and really consider: what are all of your options? So often we stop ourselves by only seeing one or two possible paths to follow, when really there are many more. Be as free and imaginative as you can with your thinking. Do not stop to consider logistics or other people, and put the choices you come up with into each arm of the cross. When I devised this exercise, I seemed to have issues around categories such as job, fun, family, home environment, finances, and my body. I felt frozen in the discontent that surrounded each of these categories. I couldn't see any options, and I feared what I might find, or not find, if I dared to take a step out of the conflict. But then I read something that Maya Angelou said. She sees each possible road as simply another adventure, and she suggests that we are meant to try as many paths as we want. If one or another doesn't turn out to be to our liking, than we need only return to the center and go down another road. Scratch the surface of anything and opportunity bubbles up. Our dreams can stay alive only if we continue to journey. Perpetual movement and curiosity will eventually bring you to your intended destiny. It is time to set out and relish your uncharted territory.

When you have filled in your cross, challenge yourself to try each of the paths you have marked. You just never know which one will truly lead you through the crossroads. Part of the trick with this exercise is to free yourself up to envision possible options and, equally important, to turn your attitude around so that every choice is welcomed as an opportunity for adventure.

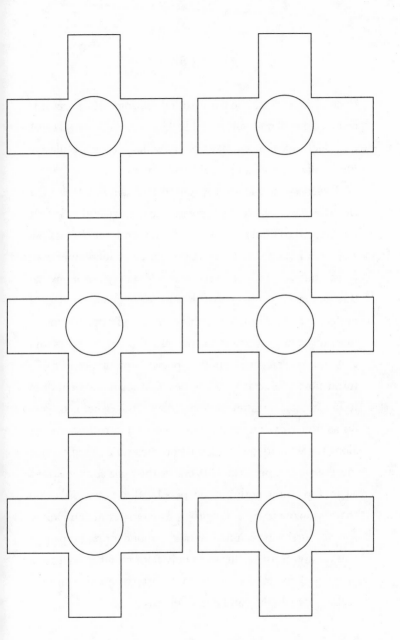

187

Being Bold

Even if we can see the paths to follow, some of us feel surrounded by people who are blocking our progress. To get past such hurdles, we have to be willing to create ultimatums, take a stand, and be viewed as not nice.

Recently I had an exchange with a cousin in which I felt that she was both angrily aggressive and judgmental. At first I attempted to hold my ground and stay with the discussion, and then I simply shut up. Although I felt incredibly confused and hurt, I also realized that it is simply not in my nature anymore to be either hostile or judgmental—that I prefer to have a discourse, share ideas and opposing opinions, and, I hope, learn in the process. But I also understand that you can't change another person's nature—you can't, for instance, force someone to be a Christian and believe in Jesus Christ, no matter how important your belief is to you. So as you grow and change you are bound to lose people along the way. In long-term relationships we easily get stuck in habits and expectations. We have the same conversations again and again with certain people. But every now and then, we have to be willing to update our scripts and allow people, ourselves included, to talk, respond, or participate in a new way. Relationships can only flourish when there is a meeting of the minds—when each party wants to continue seeking, developing, and eventually evolving.

Erin Brockovich's bold advice makes the point: "If you're not pissing a few people off, raising a few eyebrows, you're not living big enough." Once I took her sentiments to heart, it became easier for me to begin the process of living big, leaving more than a few persons on the wayside. Many weekend retreaters use the euphoria they feel on Sunday to become very bold once they return home. Rachel told her gambling husband to get help for his addiction or get out; DeeDee, who had moved unwillingly with her husband, decided to move back to the town they had just left, to paint and be closer to her friends; Susannah left her not-good-for-her married lover and took a job in a neighboring state, away from the temptation of this addictive relationship; Pam quit her six-figure job and opened a small nursery and herb garden; Maria started saying no to sex unless she desired it enough to initiate it. All of these women knew that in order to gain the freedom they needed and wanted, they first needed to make a bold move.

Some retreaters face subtler and more personal hurdles in their quest to move forward. They might need to cease messing with anyone else's future; or have the desire to live more abundantly rather than carefully; or feel an interest in exploring unconventional choices regardless of other people's reactions. The important thing is that, when you commit yourself to reinventing your life, when you accept that you have begun your second journey, then you must act with courage and begin to remove whatever blocks your newly sought-after path.

What do you get when you dare to see all of your choices and follow out the ones that speak to you alone? What happens when you stand up for yourself and decide to live boldly? You begin to realize that your dreams are possible. You find a new sense of purpose. You become buoyant and alive. As Goethe once said, "Reach for the fullness of human life—if you but touch it, it will fascinate. We live it all, but few live it knowingly."

END OF CHAPTER SUMMARY

· Diagram all your options

· Live boldly

· Choose to follow your passions—however large or small

· Collect compliments

Small but Powerful Journeys

Second journeys come in all sizes and shapes—and they are not measured by mountain peaks scaled or marathons run. Small journeys can have just as significant an impact on the overall course and tone of your life. It's all about embracing unpredictability—creatively disengaging from your typical day and the people with whom you live, to follow your instincts, whatever form they may take. Any activity has the potential to become fertile ground for growth. New involvements especially revivify your intellectual, emotional, spiritual, and physical outlook. In the process, they also illuminate unexpected paths.

When Joan Erikson first discovered modern dance, she became almost giddy. "I can do this, I can obviously do this," she exclaimed to anyone who would listen. "What a wonderful thing to make use of every part of my body." She had always had the hunch that her body was her strength and that she could do more with it than produce babies or accomplish her daily tasks. "Dance helped me along—away from the rules," Joan explained to me. "It's fluid. It makes you more flexible and physical and therefore willing for life! When you are dancing you are expressing with your whole body what you don't have words for, and in time, you get to sheer ecstasy."

A friend of mine felt the same type of delight when she went back to being a serious artist. "Oh, I taught art in the local high school, but I could never find enough time to do justice to a full-blown painting career of my own. When the kids left home, I created a studio in one of their bedrooms and began painting. I found that I simply couldn't stop. Not only did I recently hang my first-ever one-woman show, but a friend and I have developed a program for women to rediscover themselves through art, journaling, memoir, and body work. I feel as if I have found a place for me in my life, and I am driven to encourage others to find their way out of stagnation." Her excitement has been so infectious that even her husband has been drawn into her work. During her art opening, he shook his head in amazement at the crowds and energy and happily put "sold" stickers on numerous paintings.

Most of us long for wholeness. We long to unearth those raw-material resources that we own but simply haven't had a chance, or the courage, to use. You must literally begin again and again over the course of a lifetime. You can't really know what it is you are supposed to do unless you take the time to experiment with this and that and then refire your spirit. Experimentation is the only way out of stagnation.

We all have special inclinations, individual ideas, a certain "take" on things. When we come to a point, finally, where we don't brush these away as nonsense, then we give ourselves the chance to find out what truly makes us happy. Second journeys begin with a hunch, an inkling, a desire to reverse a bad situation. They develop when we follow these intimations of happiness and dare to explore who we ourselves truly are.

Some of the more obvious second journeys involve well-known people. Jimmy Carter had to start from scratch after losing reelection to the presidency, asking the same question we are asking: What am I to do or be now? After many false starts and hours of soul-searching, he started building one house at a time and spearheaded Habitat for Humanity. Mother Teresa came to feel that her life as a single woman was meaningless. She detested feeling the dilettante, and eagerly accepted her "call" to the church. So it was that, at age forty, she commenced her second journey and founded an order of nuns dedicated to serving the poorest of the poor in India.

The quest for an authentic existence is worth every ounce of effort, because the rewards will affect not only you but also all those around you. Psychologist Douglas LaBier, an expert on adult love, believes that each partner in a couple must leave the relationship, figuratively or literally, in order to find his or her gift or bliss, and then return with a newfound energy that will reignite the relationship itself. Long-term relationships need new energy, which they can get when either partner grows or changes.

Indeed, after my year of soul-searching, my husband saw the rewards I had gained and wanted some for himself. Rather than watching from the sidelines, he jumped into his own search for adventures and new vocations. He went from being a volunteer in the town to becoming an elected official, from being a statewide school inspector to becoming the interim president of a college. As my writing career flourished, so did his life. We both found ourselves participating in new areas, and the excitement we felt invigorated our marriage.

"You cannot travel on the path before you have become the

path," said Gautama Buddha. Becoming productive and proactive in both small and large ways adds color to your life, like a crocus popping up from under a blanket of white snow. Getting started on a path brings contentment and a sense of rising hope. Indeed, taking action, any action, proves that there is more to life than simply contemplating or thinking about things. One path leads to another; we reignite feelings of intensity and passion that have been lying dormant for too long. We also begin to notice that we are having fun along the way.

So go for it—anything. Take a step beyond the familiar. Who knows where a painting class might lead, or what taking up belly-dancing will do for your happiness and goals, or training for a bike race, or simply deciding to read one book a month in a different subject area. Being a scholar of self and soul is ongoing. The most significant way to keep "studying" is to explore all the possibilities available. Along the way, one interest will speak to you, and your own unique second journey will begin. We all owe it to ourselves to cultivate a full life. We all have the strength and creativity to build something out of nothing. Besides, as Joan Erikson would say, "It's a weakness to just sit around and wait for life to come to you." It does not take an inordinate amount of energy to live creatively. All that we need to redesign our lives is to move toward those values that we have come to see as the most meaningful and life-sustaining. What we seek, seeks us.

SECOND-JOURNEY QUESTIONNAIRE

- Has change been thrust upon you over the past few years?

- Have you experienced a crisis of feelings?

- Have you felt the need to take an outer journey—to go away alone, to have an adventure, to be momentarily in-dependent?

- If you have done this already, did you feel a shift taking place while on that journey? Did you begin to experience a shift in regard to meaning, values, and goals?

- Do you want to leave behind old goals and values that seem meaningless or shallow in the face of where you are now?

- As a result of your shift, are you beginning to feel out of the loop, apart from your friends, and therefore some-what lost again?

To proceed to the next phase of your life, you will need to challenge yourself in a bigger way. You may need to leave your present relationship for a time, travel to an un-known foreign place, or take up a new career. You are on a new journey now, your second journey. Along the way, as you stay true to yourself, you will begin to feel a newfound sense of empowerment.

COLLECTING COMPLIMENTS

As we are setting out on our second journeys, we are constantly faced with choices about what direction to take, what interests to pursue, what relationships to continue. One of the most important choices we face is whether to listen to ourselves or to others. We cannot possibly learn to follow our own instincts if we do not feel good about ourselves, if we do not learn to silence the negative voices that always threaten to wear us down. Sometimes these voices come from others; sometimes they come from deep inside ourselves. One of the easiest ways to bolster your self-confidence is to collect compliments.

When my self-esteem was at its lowest, I went so far as to walk around repeating my virtues out loud to myself. This was my way of affirming the good qualities that I knew I possessed, but which others seemed rarely to notice. Or did they? Perhaps my husband was stingy with compliments, but was everyone else in my life stingy, too? It began to occur to me that maybe my own lack of self-esteem was at fault. In my embarrassment or disbelief, perhaps I was simply deflecting all the good things others said about me.

I decided to try to listen to others when they talked to me—to really hear what they were saying and to make note of any compliments that came along. Much to my surprise, I found myself on the receiving end of many nice comments, some from my editor, over the phone from a daughter-in-law, from friends who were serving on a charity committee with me. I took to jotting them down on Post-its and sticking them onto my computer. In time, I learned not only to listen and hear these compliments, but to believe them as well.

Regaining self-respect and self-esteem is possible if we listen more to the positive comments that surround us and ignore, or stop dwelling on, the negative. Compliments can become clues to what you are good at and in which direction you might want to head. So take the time to listen to what others have to say, believe the good stuff, and act on it.

Return

Decide to Be New
in an Old Place

"We come into life to give certain gifts.
If we don't give them, who else will? We are so unique,
individual—it would be a precious gift lost to the world
if we didn't share."

ANONYMOUS

Re-entry

All good things must come to an end, and, alas, so does a weekend away. But that doesn't mean you should quickly drop back into your old life and not hang on to every last morsel of serenity and insight you have gained on retreat. After all, the very point of retreating is to repair, regenerate, and return—not merely refreshed, but changed. Once you sit back and take stock, you realize that, really, everything has shifted—the way you look, the way you behave, the way you feel, the way you think. In order to hold on to this wonderful, unfinished woman you have grown into, you must remain enlightened. And that can only happen if you take your re-entry as seriously as you took your leavetaking.

I'll never forget Delilah, a gorgeous thirty-something woman from New York City. Delilah had a huge career in banking, a husband, two small children, and several assistants. But when she was in dire need of time out, she left them all behind in order to retreat on the Cape. From the minute she walked into the inn, everyone felt her confidence. Her body language asserted a sense of control and power; her questions were to the point; her determination to shift and grow was resolute. As the weekend progressed, she marched ahead, seeming to absorb the experience effortlessly and change with every experience. But then, Sunday afternoon, while all the others basked in the sun and their own euphoria, Delilah struggled to hold back her tears. In a sheepish voice she finally asked: "How do I go home and re-enter my life after this? I am so frightened."

It was the first time anyone had ever directly asked that question, and I felt hard-pressed for a good answer. Re-entry is a tricky time. It is much more complicated than initially meets the eye, and it is certainly one of the most anxiety-provoking parts of the weekend program. I suggested to Delilah that she take it moment to moment, with no preconceived plan. She looked puzzled and obviously disappointed that I didn't have a more concrete answer. She was looking for and in fact needed a plan.

"But I know my husband will be full of questions," she insisted.

"Of course he will," I continued, "but right now you have no answers."

"What?" she asked, and everyone else in the room seemed just as startled. Hadn't they just spent an entire weekend asking questions of themselves, pondering their pasts and futures, looking for meaning in nature's metaphors? How could they not be going home with a plethora of strategies?

"Right now," I continued, "you are full of feelings and the memory of experiences, but you can't possibly have processed it all. Experiencing an 'aha' moment is one thing. Making total sense of all of such moments and then articulating your new knowledge to others is quite another. It took me several years to figure out how I had changed and how to explain it to my family and friends. Truly you have shifted, but it would behoove you not to try and share how just now. Keep your experiences to yourself for a little while. Revisit them. Muse on their meaning and significance. Hold tight to your new goals and dreams. When you blurt out all your new thoughts to those who wait for you at home, you risk losing some of your newfound power. They haven't done the work, or had the inclination to ask the deep questions, and most likely they will feel threatened by your answers and try to argue against your new values. For the moment, it is best to say something simple like: 'It was amazing, but I haven't quite figured it out yet. When I do, I'll let you know.' "

Slow Down, Don't Move Too Fast

I liken re-entry to the blackout period experienced by astronauts when they plummet back toward the earth's atmosphere after a space flight. During this time, there is no communication between Mission Control and the space vehicle—there is, instead, *a pause*—a moment when quiet overtakes everyone involved, until the spacecraft finally, securely lands.

A similar pause can help a retreater extend the feelings felt and process the insight gained on retreat. My own husband always thought a pause was important when he came home from work. If he could walk in the door, go off to the bedroom, change his clothes, and breathe, he knew he could then contribute to the family during the rest of the evening. We need to give ourselves this same respect before, during, and even after we return to our home bases in order to continue the exhilarating journey we have begun.

I have a friend, Lynne, who took it upon herself to care for a neighbor who was dying of AIDS. His family had abandoned him, and Lynne not only nursed him but also planned his funeral—all this while continuing to care for her own two small children. As she walked into her house after the burial, drained and heavy with her unprocessed grief, her husband confronted her in a terribly insensitive manner: "So—are you finally back?" he asked. "Ready to be our wife and mother again?" Lynne fell to pieces. She was physically incapable of walking right back into the roles she had temporarily stepped away from without some time to process her sadness, gather up her strength, and then, only then, prepare to rejoin her family. Of course, Lynne desperately needed to nap, but she also needed to grieve her loss—to pause attentively—just as do all women as they begin any re-entry.

The weekend retreaters have become very creative about re-entry. Many return home, but not to work—taking a few days alone in their houses to reacclimate. Two friends who came from just outside of Boston deliberately took the long way home. They bicycled along the Cape Cod Canal and then stopped at a favorite restaurant for a gourmet dinner. When they finally pulled into their driveways, their families were in bed and they were able to adjust in silence and darkness. Other retreaters have taken a motel room on a whim, just to give themselves one more night of freedom; and many simply extend their stay at our little inn until it feels right to leave.

One young retreater used her re-entry pause, a long flight back to Idaho, to read and reread a letter she'd written to herself in her journal:

Dear Elaine:

Darling, you do have the time. You know that, yes? One cannot rush these eight gifts of Hope, Purpose, Confidence, Fidelity, Love, Care, and Wisdom. They show themselves when they are ready—but I will give you more specific tools, as I know you better than you know yourself.

Do not explain, convince, justify, or manipulate others! You now know how to affirm yourself. Affirming is not an issue of being greedy or selfish. You are capable of blessing, affirming, recognizing, and approving yourself! I know this because I know you!

Understand that everything will be OK. Ha! you say. Too simple? No. Breathe. You are thirty-six. You have approximately 528 months to live, give or take a few. You are happy now? It only gets better. I know because I know your future. Oh yeah, I do. Your job is to raise those two children so that they don't need to depend on you anymore. Everything will only get better and better. You have the tools. You know what you need to do, but breathe.

Accept responsibility. What is the worst that can happen? Rejection? Disapproval? Abandonment? Already dealt with those trite issues! You are so much stronger than you take credit for, Elaine! When you feel happiness, contentment, and peace, you have no one to blame (or credit) but yourself. The life of the moon shell is yours. Do what makes you feel good (within reason) and accept responsibility! Approval and affirmation from outside sources CANNOT work anymore. Do not depend on that external pulse. You want YOUR power back? You already have it, Girlfriend!

NooOooOooOooGUILT! Guilt just excuses you from not doing what you think others want you to do. Do not feel guilty! What is guilt? You know your limitations. Now start living. The clock is ticking. Have fun!

I love you.

Elaine

Elaine's reacclimation to home was relatively uneventful. By staying with her thoughts, she was able to solidify her new perspective and attitude and really find firm footing before anyone could get to her and upset her balance. "I returned home with a secret inner peace, a new sense of calm that I owned. I felt closer to myself and stronger, too—not so dependent—self-sufficient, actually. I knew I could take care of the big things like finances and health insurance if I had to, because during the weekend I had gotten to know all of my strengths."

Secrets Are Power

Elaine instinctively followed the advice of the writer Louise Driscoll, who says, "Within your heart, keep one, still spot where dreams may go." She used her pause to tuck her new sense of her own strength and power into her heart, where it could remain protected from the challenges of her daily life and the demands of her young family.

Joan Erikson first taught me the power of secrets—of holding on to information or fresh thoughts until they become a part of you. "Secrets are our power, dear," she used to say. "They give you a chance to try things out in the privacy of your individual space. It has always been my game to have secrets. Having a secret develops a strong personality. It turns frustration into power, somehow. I love to do things and tell about them much later, if at all. I suppose I started this because most of the stuff I did as a child was not approved of. I just had to get on with my adventures, and living my own life, in secret. All those piled-up secrets became my individuality."

Joan urged me to explore any world that interested me, setting just one rule or goal—be home in time for dinner. "Most people around you are so self-absorbed that they hardly care what you are up to—that is, until your new life threatens to upset their apple cart. Don't tell anyone what you are up to, because they will only try to change or limit your new behavior."

Like anything else we do, when we set out to change habits and behavior it is best to start small and in private. No point in heralding your intentions; you may simply end up scaring away those around you who aren't ready to reimagine the limits of their world. Rather, simply begin to implement change one step at a time. A little new behavior goes a long way toward achieving balance. The hope is that while on retreat you learned what you need to make your day pleasant (and remember, pleasant is the goal—we have had enough of trying to be perfect). Practice pleasant days and trust that the bigger changes will follow.

I always make sure that I have taken some action, done some bodywork, had a good amount of contemplative time, and played with fresh thoughts. By making sure such pleasures are in my day, I become my own personal coach—I hire my own consciousness to keep me action-oriented and involved. This is my formula for high maintenance. One step begets another, and before you know it the mundane moments of the past have become delightful days of your present.

Remaining Enlightened

The more you challenge yourself, the less fearful you will be of the regard and judgment of others. Family and friends will either join you or fall away. But as you continue along the road less traveled, those around you will eventually see your commitment to change—you are in motion and there is no stopping you.

Your deviations from the old routines will begin to feel normal, not extreme. With each conscious new endeavor, you will be inspired just a little bit more. "When a woman senses that there is a mythic dimension to something she is undertaking," says Jean Shinoda Bolen, "that knowledge touches and inspires a deep creative center within her." Before you know it, she will be soaring.

This is certainly what happened to Denise, the retreater who was moved to follow her dream and work for a time in East Africa. From the moment she arrived at the airport and boarded her plane for her adventure, she felt at utter peace. "I was so calm—sure, like never before, of what I was doing. And once in Africa, working with children, observing the strength of the women—how they endured, indeed thrived on little or nothing—my resolve to stay the course and continue on my new path became even stronger."

With a fiery directness, Denise now continues to seek more adventure and use her skills as a social worker in other needy places. All those hurdles she worried about scaling have fallen out of sight. Nothing can deter her. She is in love with the idea that she has indeed earned the right to live a full existence. And why not? For, as Irish philosopher John O'Donohue says in his book of Celtic wisdom:

> *Deep within every life, no matter how dull or ineffectual it may seem, something eternal is happening. When you are faithful to the risk and ambivalence of growth, you are engaging your life. The soul loves risk; it is only through the door of risk that growth can enter. Possibility and change become growth within the shape of time that we call our*

day. Days are where we live. The rhythm shapes our lives. Each new day offers possibilities that were never seen before. To engage with honor the full possibility of your life is to engage in a worthy way the possibility of your new day.

So there you have it. To remain enlightened, you must accept your own essential holiness. Decide on how to shape your day so that in the end you have some focus and control around it. As I said earlier, I need action, bodywork, and time for contemplative thought in order to continue being the conscious person I now choose to be. What is it you need to maintain your new, finely tuned, purposeful life? It may just be some significant moments. For, as an eighty-five-year-old friend of mine said recently: "Oh, I've had my moments, and if I had it to do over again, I'd have more of them. In fact, I'd try to have nothing else—just moments, one after another, instead of living so many years ahead of each day."

Salty Sisters

Up until your return, your work has been done mostly in solitude and internally, but in order to continue your journey, you will need to find people who welcome your desire to change and nurture your new ideals. None of us can go it alone; it really does take a village to stay the course, and I recommend to all of my retreaters that when they have found their rhythm again they form a women's circle. Jungian Jean Shinoda Bolen suggests the same in her book *The Millionth Circle* when she claims that the only way to change ourselves (and subsequently the world) is to form a circle.

Many past retreaters have found that they can hold on to the good cheer of the weekend by keeping in contact with each other. I recently went to visit one particularly organized group of past retreaters who call themselves the Salty Sisters. These women instinctively reached for each other at the end of their weekend retreat, and their story is inspiring.

> *Just two years ago, I attended a Weekend by the Sea. I often describe that weekend as the single most important event in my now forty-nine years, because during that time, I gave birth to myself. Twenty-two strangers from across the country witnessed that birth. Nine of those strangers have become my best friends, my Salty Sisters.*
>
> *When the weekend ended, the nine of us knew that we needed to keep in touch, and so we pledged to travel by plane and car to visit each other four times a year, to continue the personal journeys we'd begun on Cape Cod, and to cultivate our wild and salty womanhood. These reunions have kept me going and focused on improving my life.*
>
> *We first came together out of pain and ache and sor-*

row, and now we stay together for hope, and questions, and dreams. With each other, we explore our connections to family and friends, our role in our lives, and the workings of our personalities. We pull apart big questions like "What's the difference between being in love and loving someone?" Or "How do I mother my grown children?" We work to our own aches and fears and dreams, we applaud and cheer and cry for each other, we explore and search for intent and purpose. And by doing all this, we validate each other and our individual selves as women. Our commitment to each other is intense because it is a commitment we've made to ourselves.

Four times a year, sometimes more, we gather in a different town or vacation spot. We rent a house rather than visit each other, because not one of us wants to play hostess. We spend most of our time just talking, sharing our vast and varied experience, and catching up on whatever events have affected us. There is always someone to offer advice or counsel, be it emotional, spiritual, medical, or legal. We eat, we bike, and we read. We don't follow a schedule, and we have fun.

In between these reunions, we e-mail each other constantly. Every morning when I turn on my computer, I find that one of my Salty Sisters has already checked in to say "Good morning." When a crisis erupts for any one of us, we clamor together and offer as much sympathy, advice, *and prayer as we can. Even though we live all over, I always feel that I am part of a very tight, close, supportive community.*

I have found that these are the only people in my life who I can be with without needing time away. That is because we have shared and honored the private parts of ourselves with each other. Our bond is reciprocal, giving and receiving, full of honesty and love. We retreat and repair, we regenerate and release, and when we return to our homes, we re-enter with support. The Salty Sisterhood is a tool that helps me stay on my path toward self-empowerment, growth, and self-love. It is a tool that helps me maintain my balance, focus, and clarity. The bond of the Salty Sisters goes beyond good friendship. As Salty Sisters, we sponsor each other in our individual quests to sponsor ourselves. For all of this, I am beyond grateful.

The Salty Sisters banded together for the express purpose of empowering each other. Subconsciously they knew that they would need some auxiliary support as they re-entered their lives—an undergirding to help bolster their newfound intentions and desires. The security and trust they inspire in each other were lacking in most of their other friendships, in which old habits, old ways of talking and responding, stifled their new desire to change. But with each other, everything is open for conversation. As one of them explained to me recently, "No matter how reluctant you might be to share something with the group, a secret, sexual advice, health issues, marriage issues, there are no limits. With each other, we are fully ourselves."

Create Your Own Lifeline

In order to keep your sight on your ever-increasing goals, and to resist the tease to slip back into your outdated life, you, too, will need to surround yourself with supportive women. The objective of any woman who has begun to take back her life is to learn to live more creatively, and a network of support can help you feel secure enough to accept new challenges, try out new adventures, and continue to redefine the shape and quality of your existence.

The ancient Greeks believed that, through constant dialogue and honest sharing, friends could reach a higher level of truth together, and women, especially, have gathered from time immemorial to whisper, share, and console. Old-time quilting bees, for example, were as much about patching up lives as they were about stitching together pieces of fabric. As they sewed, the women quilters talked, sharing their pains, their joys, and their wisdom, helping one another fit all the pieces together, and reinforcing seams. Even today, in our hectic existence, women still feel the need to connect and share. We just do it on the run—at PTA meetings, in the ladies' room, during power walks, or before and after book club.

The Salty Sisters were fortunate to have already met each other and shared their feelings and experiences over the course of their weekend retreat. Most of you will need to start a circle of friends on your own. This should not be a daunting task. Like-minded women are magnetically drawn to each other. You need only begin a pursuit of one dream or try out a longed-for endeavor and you will suddenly find kindred spirits all around. As Phoebe, one of the Salty Sisters, explains:

> *You simply have to recognize the ache. There is almost a leap of faith that you must take to realize that you are not alone with your ache. You need to risk putting it out there to bring like-minded people to you. For example, the summer before my oldest boy went to college, I experienced a huge ache. It was a huge feeling of emptiness. All I could think of to do was send out a flyer to women who must be feeling like me. I went through the high-school directory and sent out fifty flyers. Thirty-four women came to my house—women who had never met before—to laugh, cry, and commiserate about the meaning of change in their homes and lives. We have given our group a name—the MT Club, which meant "My Time." Once we got together, we realized it was no longer about being empty, but*

about taking our turn. Today, some two years later, our core group numbers twenty. We meet the third Tuesday each month, just to celebrate ourselves.

It also helps to have a specific focus. Fifteen years ago, I gathered a diverse group of women to study *Women Who Run With the Wolves.* Over the course of a year, we read the book and talked about our spirits, bodies, intellectual and emotional capacities, and relationships. We cried, loved, shouted, and listened. When we finished the book, we continued to gather. Just like the Salty Sisters, or the MT Club, these women have helped me navigate all the twists and turns in my life. They support my decisions and feelings without judgment. Most important, they buoy me to continue to challenge the scripted roles and all the "shoulds" society throws out as direction. Together we have changed our lives and our families, for, as Margaret Mead once said, "Never doubt that a small group of thoughtful, committed citizens can change the world—indeed it is the only thing that ever has."

Lifeline Steps

1. Recognize a particular ache

2. Know that you are not alone

3. Stick your neck out and share your feelings

4. Choose a format and shape for your group

5. Commit to meeting regularly

Be Generative

Besides the necessary pause, the ability to keep a secret, and support from like-minded souls who will continue to cheer you on, a successful re-entry requires that you find a way to be generative. You may recall that, just after I spent my year alone by the sea, a group of friends came to visit and wanted to know the steps I had followed. With Joan Erikson's encouragement, I turned my experience into a series of memoirs. Each book I wrote helped me to stay connected with all that I had learned about sponsoring myself and listening to my own inner voice. I had found a way to be generative, to pass on the wisdom I had gained, and to encourage more and more women to appreciate all that is unfinished in their lives.

"Each one teach one," said Dr. Albert Schweitzer, who brought modern medicine to the bush in Africa, and Joan Erikson certainly would have agreed with his mantra. "Reciprocity is awfully important," she said time and time again. "There is no growth and change without involvement and interaction. Solitude is still the place where it all comes together and finally makes the most sense for you. But it is in the living and the passing on of our experiences that new actions and attitudes set down firm roots."

There are many ways to be generative. Some of the women retreaters have returned home and started book clubs with their friends in which they read books that encourage them to discuss the ongoing growth. Others have returned for additional weekends accompanied by daughters or nieces. I found a way to be generative and mentor other women beyond the writing of my books when I joined a local charity that rescues women in crisis through financial aid and counseling. As Toni Morrison said, "If you have some power, your job is to empower somebody else."

Joan was amazing in this aspect of her living. She would never give direct advice per se. She simply exuded an energy that was contagious. You couldn't be a slug in her presence—you wanted to be as active and involved as she was. Up until the day she died, she stayed vitally involved, questing, creating, and supporting anything in which she believed. What's more, she did it all with playfulness as much as dignity. She was proud to be a "grown-down," and almost always surrounded herself with people thirty or forty years younger, because they could offer another perspective—some new morsel to chew on.

You don't need a specific cause; simply commit yourself to remaining involved and enthusiastic. During your various adventures, you will suddenly reach a point when you feel courageous rather than desperate. Others will see that courage. When you least expect it, your energy and spirit will excite someone else's, and you will have become an inspiration. The quest for an authentic life is full of effort and full of rewards, but it isn't worth a damn unless you pass it on.

"As long as life is possible, hang on to it, scoop it up, keep your hands on the plow!" That was Joan's charge, and now I bequeath it on to you. When the call comes, answer it. When the doorway opens, however unexpectedly, cross over the threshold. You become the heroine of your own story only if you are willing to risk—to continue to journey, to believe that the daring is doable. This book cannot offer all the answers, but it is written with the conviction that you are up to the task. Know that as you move forward you will be offered myriad signs of hope, courage, and confidence.

Recently, at an ultramarathon, I witnessed a sixty-eight-year-old woman crossing the finish line. When I asked why she ran in hundred-mile races, she said: "Because I am a woman, and women endure. My message is that there is no limit to a woman's endurance." We are all part of an endurance contest—the run of our lives. But I also like to think we are part of a relay race—we all carry our unique torches in hopes of one day passing them on to the hand in front of us, to the woman poised and ready to run her leg of the race.

Your glass is no longer half empty, but half full. The question becomes: how are you going to continue to fill it up—to fill out your life cycle?

Once you have found yourself, there is no going back. Periodic retreat, retrieval, repair, regrouping, regeneration, and re-entry will continue to help you stay the course. What's more, you will never return to the way you were, because you've:

Tasted too much of the other

Realized how lonely it is if you aren't all one

Come to enjoy being your own heroine

Taken the necessary time with transitions—grieving and letting go

Moved beyond the roles to a real self

Fallen in love with your unconditional life style

As my yoga instructor says at the end of every class:

Namaste. I honor in you the divine that I honor within myself and I know that we are one.

END OF CHAPTER SUMMARY

· Pause

· Keep some of your intentions secret

· Organize a circle of female seekers

· Be generative

· Pass on the torch

Connecting the Dots

"Nothing is worth more than this day."

GOETHE

A lot of women have called me brave, and for the longest time, I had a tremendous amount of difficulty accepting that compliment. They said I was brave to have taken a stand, brave to have run away, brave to have lived by myself, brave to have looked deeply at my messy life, brave to write about it. But brave to me is someone who faces a terminal illness, stands up to a philandering husband, or rebuilds after some sort of natural disaster. Nothing I've done has ever come close to that type of bravery. So, when someone called me brave, I usually rushed to efface myself.

But then, one day, I finally said, "You're right. I suppose you could say there was some modicum of bravery in what I did to shake up my life and stand by my impulsive words even though I had no idea how the separation would turn out." At the time, I certainly felt more desperate than brave. I became rash because I could no longer allow my days simply to happen. I needed a new approach. And although it may have appeared to many that I was just running away, I somehow felt pregnant with possibilities and in need of giving birth to all of my latent potentials. One moment of impulse, one moment of listening to an inner whisper, one moment, I have learned, can indeed change your life.

Perhaps I was fortunate to have an inciting incident to get me to move off the dime. When my husband announced what he was about to do, I instantly knew what I needed. Following the leader was simply not going to cut it anymore. I wanted my autonomy, my originality, my very self back. In an instant, I knew that it was my turn—my turn to engage in my own life, to individuate again, despite having done so when I left my parents' home and again when my sons left our home. It's humorous, actually, how we fight change and hold on to cherished notions and old habits rather than jump into the uncertainty of the challenges and adventures that lie ahead. Taking action is rarely easy for any of us. Yet, as M. Scott Peck once said, "It is in the whole process of meeting and solving problems that life has meaning. Life is difficult, but it is only through mastering the challenges that we get to the meaning." I began to change my life the moment I stood in the middle of the problem and impulsively, bravely, daringly chose to act in a new way. The truth is that any woman can be this brave.

So, nine years later, how have I changed? For one thing, I know now that I belong right in the middle of every dilemma. The solution to my problems is not to avoid them, or to follow a scripted response. I need to have enough confidence, enough self-respect, enough bravery to meet each challenge head-on and pursue an original solution. I need to trust the present moment to guide me by listening to my feelings and desires, whatever they may be. I need to pursue my dreams so that I can encourage others to pursue theirs. Not small goals, any of them. But I am determined—I am woman—I am invincible, as the song says.

My new attitude is captured in a sentiment of Goethe's that is inscribed on a mug I sip my coffee from each morning: "Nothing is worth more than this day." My life changed when I learned to concentrate on little moments. It is during the little moments rather than the big ones that I learn the most. Little moments contain all the wisdom, all the truth, all the pleasure that I need to continue to grow. And when I focus my attention on those little and simple moments, I can filter out all the distracting static created by the voices that urge me to do this or that. Collect little moments.

Last summer, it was my oldest son's children who taught me the importance of Goethe's thought as they tumbled into our bed at the crack of dawn, each morning—feet damp from running across the dewy lawn from their cottage to ours. This summer, in particular, was one of those rare perfect summers—just the right number of relatives and guests trickling through, balmy days and cool, crisp nights, special time with women friends, and grandchildren still innocent yet also finally able to take part in just about any activity. Our days typically began with three of my five grandsons nestled under our down comforter, eager for a story, either read or told. Robin and I particularly enjoyed the conversations and questions that inevitably ensued. In time, once we'd read Carson his favorite story about Jackie Robinson changing the face of baseball, answered Logan's questions about why a family of foxes live in our backyard and just how far away are the coyotes that howl in the night, and tickled Tully under each elbow and knee, we'd look out the window to check on the weather and the day's activities. Clouds meant fishing, miniature golf, or bike rides. Sun meant the beach, although which beach occasioned yet another lively discussion over breakfast—should we load up the wagon and walk to the one just down the street, or take a boat ride to wild South Beach with a picnic lunch in tow? If it was windy, perhaps we'd fly a kite, and if it was rainy, we might work on a puzzle or bake an apple pie.

Snuggled into bed with our grandchildren, I had no choice but to greet each day with love, laughter, and the wild enthusiasm children have for anything new. Even now, long after the summer is over, our grandsons' desire to dig into each day without reservation is catching. And I am continually reminded: the sock forgotten in the dryer, the shovel thrown into the flower garden, the half-eaten Popsicles left in haste on my freezer shelf, all remind me to follow the sun or the wind, to welcome the rain and the blue sky alike, to live each moment as if nothing is more important than this particular day. "And a child shall lead them," the Bible says; and so these young boys have pushed me to seize each day and pack my life with soul-filled moments, which are the most important, after all.

It is said that one conquers dullness not by moving one's body but by changing one's soul. Indeed, the Roman writer Apuleius said, "Everyone should know that you can't live in any other way than by cultivating your soul." In order to do that, you must craft, or in this case recraft, your life so that it is characterized by genuineness and depth. You must have satisfying conversation, real connections, moving music, quality time with innocent children. Soul-filled moments bring tears to our eyes, catch us off guard, make us gasp, and send warmth through our veins.

I am reminded of my younger son's wedding. His bride-to-be was an actress by profession, and it was clear to us all that this wedding would be the performance of her life. Both of them had memorized their vows, rehearsed their dance, and styled their costumes. But when the moment arrived and the priest whispered her cue, she turned toward her groom, looked deep into his eyes, and barely uttered a shaky "I, Susannah Kavanaugh," before the tears overwhelmed all of her well-rehearsed poise. As she sobbed, the sacred truth of the moment emerged—the wedding ceremony turned into an authentic happening, with palpable passion and obvious love right there for all to witness and share.

I felt doubly fortunate because, just several days before, when the family had gathered at our home to await the big day, I had the idea that it might be meaningful to do a blessing of my two sons and one daughter-in-law since Luke was about to be married, and Andy and Shelly were embarking on a long and dangerous cycling tour. A little prayerful beginning certainly couldn't harm anything. My church offered a Wednesday-morning prayer service that I asked the children to attend. They grumbled and resisted. It was too early, it was too cold, and they needed coffee and the paper before they interacted with people. Eventually, however, I won out—a mother has her ways—and off we went at the crack of dawn.

As we stood in a circle, shivering in the early-morning cold, altar candles flickering, and surrounded by strangers, I wondered what I had done. But then I gave my daughter-in-law a chalice of wine, and she turned and offered it to her husband, and he turned and offered it to his brother. Through this simple ritual, one that happened in a moment and apart from the typical stream of our day, we connected with each other and acknowledged the sacredness of our lives, our choices, and the endeavors upon which we were embarking.

Three days later, as Susannah drew her gathered friends and family into the love she and Luke felt for each other, I again felt a sacred, soulful connection to the people around me. Whole lifetimes can be built around such key moments, and I now know that *nothing is worth more than caring for our souls,* because when we care for our souls, rather than conform to our roles, we come to see that *nothing is worth more than acceptance,* both of what is and of the self.

Before my year by the sea, I felt as though I were nothing more than the roles that I played, and I couldn't accept or appreciate who I really was. I didn't have the right body, the right face, the right mind, or even the right attitude. As I drove around suburbia, working through my long list of errands, trying to please the people in my life, filling my time with doing instead of being, I would try to convince myself that I was worth more than I felt. "I am good," I would shout, and slam the steering wheel to underscore my point. "Damn, I'm good." But no matter how loudly I shouted, neither my self-image nor my self-esteem changed. I didn't learn to accept myself—not just how I look, but my original thoughts, my compassion, the way I behave—until I started caring for the quality of each day. By continuing to work the six R's I have described in this book—*retreat, repair, retrieve, regroup, regenerate,* and *return*—I am able to spiral inward and give each meaningful experience the focus it deserves.

A few years back, my older son's running career became

something that I needed to face, not fear. I needed to find a way to understand his passion for running hundred-mile races through the desert and mountains. I wanted to be able to applaud his efforts even though I thought the sport was narcissistic, addictive, and unhealthy. One summer day, when we weren't particularly getting along, he tossed a comment my way: "If you want to know who I am, Mom, then you should come to one of my runs." Aha, I thought. *Nothing is more important than acceptance of others.* So I flew across the country for the Western Endurance Run in northern California. I helped Shelly buy the supplies and pack the car. When we reached our site, I helped the kids pitch the tents we would sleep in during the race.

Andy had gone a day earlier to get his game head on, and I would not see him until he was a good twenty-five miles into the race. When he did appear, running through the forest of redwoods, looking as though he had simply run around the block, I ran out to meet him. "Mom, you made it. You're here," he said, extending his hand to me without breaking his stride. We ran together down a hill to the next station, and in that one moment my fears diminished. It was obvious he had made a science of this sport and knew precisely what both his body and his soul needed to endure. "It's the hard that makes it great," he's been known to say, and certainly sharing that little run, watching the entire experience unfold, to say nothing of seeing him run over the finish line second, made his statement all the more true. But what I really gained from the experience was acceptance—acceptance of his desire to train and run in such events, and trust that as a young adult he would do it with care and calculation.

In the past eight years, I have had to work through similar struggles with my own mother and my husband. We have all had quite a lot of adjusting to do as Robin and I figure out the next phase of our lives and Mom's health gradually declines. But through it all, I have repeated to myself, *nothing is worth more than my relationships* with friends and family. My mother deserves support and care for many reasons, not the least of which came out of the mouth of my son Luke when I complained one day that she was becoming high-maintenance. "Mom, Grandma cared for you your whole life, and so she deserves to be cared for in return." His pithy comment put an end to my complaining, that and a friend's gentle reminder of how fortunate I was to still have a mother. "I only wish I could pick up the phone once in a while and talk to mine," my friend said. "A little bit of wisdom—be sure to kiss her every time you see her. While you are at it, remember how good she smells."

Now when I have time with my mom, I make sure that I am present and focused—listening, observing, and asking her questions. Just yesterday she tied up a wayward strand of my personality by linking my devotion to hard work to an aunt, a grandmother, and a great-grandmother. She'd wanted me to be born on Sunday, a day of rest, but instead

I came on Monday, and from a very early age seemed to love pushing up my sleeves and tackling work, just like all the women in her life as they faced Monday's wash. Instantly I was imbued with a sense of history and new strength. Although I am often frustrated by the failings of her short-term memory, she's full of stories about the past and stands ready to help me connect them to my future.

As for my husband, he has worked so hard to know who he is. What a delight to live with a man who has done the work and turned up new. Together we have each been slogging through change—change in jobs, financial security, family status, health issues—and in the end we have become two individuals who are essentially remade, although we share a common history. It amazes me some days to think, as I look at him over the dinner table, I really like him! I like how he has departed from the norm and followed his heart, how he wants to give back, make a difference, carve a new path. Growing old with this man is becoming fascinating, interesting, and certainly serendipitous. "Not in his goals but in his transitions, man is great," said Emerson, and so it is for us. Growth spurts happen when we least expect them. But how wonderful when they happen at all!

Which leads me to say, *nothing is worth more than meaningful work*. At our stage of life, the work has mostly to do with fine-tuning our lives—drawing on past experience to do something meaningful in the time we have left. I was so surprised when a reader stood up at one of my bookstore appearances and said, "I think it is so interesting how you have turned your life into a vocation." Here I thought I was simply telling my story through the memoir genre. But when I got home later and looked up "vocation" in the dictionary, I saw just how right that reader was. A vocation is an inclination—an occupation for which someone is especially suited, an undertaking that comes as a result of a summons. When you take your self seriously, explore your interests, seek out wisdom, and surround yourself with like-minded souls, inevitably some kind of vocation emerges.

Finally, I have learned that *nothing thing is worth more than my own company.* Tucked away in my sacred space—Virginia Woolf really was right—taking care of my mind and spirit has proved to be more valuable than appeasing the crowd. For it is in my space, in those moments when I can sink into a dreamy idleness, that I can truly practice being the new me. It seems as if I have entered a new age—the age of re-enchantment—where I thrive on discovery, diversity, variety, spontaneity, and most days are self-directed, not programmed by invitations and obligations but, rather, determined by impulse, chance encounters, on-the-spot decisions, bravery, and new adventures, one after another.

As Emerson said: "What lies behind us and what lies before us are small matters compared to what lies within us."

Alone with my own company, I now almost always know what in my life is working and what isn't, what is sacred and therefore important, and what is irrelevant. I guess you could say all the soul-searching has brought me home to a comfortable spot in my own existence.

A Jump-Start Agenda for
a Weekend to Change Your Life

This agenda works for an individual or a group of women.

Pre-Retreat

After reading the first chapter, "Wake-up Sister. It's Your Turn," and doing the calendar exercise on page 25, plot your escape. Pick a good time to go away, and find a suitable location. Whether it is a campground, a cottage, a B & B, or an inn, it should have access to a forest, beach, state park—a place where you can also have a meaningful solo adventure.

If possible, leave on Thursday in order to get through the actual traveling. Take the evening to set up shop—haul in groceries (if needed), get comfortable in your setting, and then celebrate the fact that you got away. When was the last time? Ever?

Friday Morning (Retreat)

This is to be a day of introspection, a day for you to look backward before you move forward. Read the chapter, "Selfhood Begins by Walking Away," and then explore your immediate surroundings. Look for your sense of place—a spot that calls to you, a place that feels inviting and soothing, where you will want to return again and again during the weekend to regroup and center yourself. It could be a bench under a tree, a gazebo, a dune, or a log beside a rippling stream. It is here that you will *be still* and *listen*— where you will journal and get in touch with your senses. Once you have located your place, study where you are, notice everything that inhabits this spot; become familiar with it so that it can act as your refuge.

Now take the time to recognize your *ache*—what it means to be on empty. Know that you are in the process of replenishing yourself, but first you must understand just what you are seeking, what you are yearning for, what you need to eliminate from your life, and what you need to have more of. Ponder the transition questionnaire on pages 45–46. Once you've answered the questions, you will understand better why you needed to retreat.

Journal your thoughts using the following three sentences as starters:

"I'm lost enough to find myself."

"Change occurs when we stop living the expected life."

"There is no higher calling than to make a new creation out of the old self."

Friday Afternoon and Evening (Retrieve)

Read the next chapter "Put Yourself Back Together Piece by Piece." Spend your time doing the snapshot exercise, life-cycle logic, and the colors of your life on pages 77–79, 79–82, and 82–84. Then reflect on this statement by Oprah Winfrey: "I've learned to rely on the strengths I inherited from all those who came before me . . . the grandmothers, sisters, aunts and brothers whose spirit was tested with unimaginable hardships, yet they survived."

If you are with friends, share your thoughts about various relatives. Write down characteristics they owned that you might like to unearth. Look for your sturdy roots, and, by evening's end, revel in your newfound "relative ability."

Saturday (Repair)

Read the chapter "Turn up the Silence, Turn Down the Voices." After a hearty breakfast, head off for your three-to-four-hour solo adventure. Take with you essentials such as water, snacks, and your journal—anything you might need during the day so that you won't feel pressed to return before you are ready.

Before heading out, answer the questions in "Lighten Your Load" on pages 101–2 in order to rid yourself of psychic baggage and negative voices. This is the day to become reacquainted with yourself, to spiral inward, to center down, focus just on self, and to hear what your heart has been trying to tell you. As you move on to your wild place, think about the following sentiments:

"Make silence your friend."

"Nature teaches us the dignity of being without motive."

"Powerful messages are available in places where strife is more common than peace, where impermanence reigns, for all that lives is subject to change and erasure."

Once in your natural surroundings, begin to explore and feel a kinship with your environment. Now is the time to sweat it out, test your limits, go where you might not have ever dared. If there is a mountain to climb, climb it; if there is a river to forge, forge it. If you feel like swimming naked in a pond or the ocean, go for it. Challenge not only your mind, but also your body. Get out of your head and into your body, and be as active as possible—be like a child again, or a risky teen, anything but the careful person you are now. You are meant to cry, scream, laugh, be silly—and in so doing, process the grief that is partner to change.

Along your way, look for metaphors in nature that reflect on your life. Journal your thoughts. Eventually you might want to actually have a scavenger hunt for your soul. Look for such things as a stone that speaks, an object that is finished, a sound that stirs, an unexpected sight, something that is alive, and whatever else captures your individual imagination.

When, at the end of the day, you return to your place of retreat, spread out all the things you found in nature and journal their meaning for you. Savor the evening—get outside to look at the stars, sip wine, light candles, and indulge.

Sunday Morning (Regroup and Regenerate)

Read the chapter "Body and Soul." Begin the day reflecting on how well your body maintained you during your solo adventure. Reflect on its virtues over a cup of coffee and answer the "End of Body Bashing" questions on page 135.

Then take some time to greet the day, have a good breakfast, and eventually do the balance wheel, a helpful chart that will make it possible for you to give as much to yourself as you do to others once you return home. Factor in a walk, run, or bike ride to invigorate you. Before lunch, read the chapter "Surrender Everyone Else's Expectations."

Next do the "Give and Take Questionnaire" on pages 169–70 to ensure that you will continue to give to yourself that which you give to everyone else. This will help you stay the course.

Sunday Afternoon (Return)

Read the chapter "Gather Your Strength and Sponsor Yourself." It is time to set the stage for your re-entry as you decide to be new in an old place. The first thing you must do is diagram your choices by filling out several of the cross-road crosses on page 187.

Next formulate an intention. Choose your intention from the characteristics you recalled about your ancestors. Perhaps you want to be more rebellious, fun-loving, risky, silly, unconventional, or outrageous. Whatever you choose, find a rock or use something you brought back from your solo adventure, and write that intention where it is visible. This will be your reminder to continue to stretch toward a new way of being.

Read the chapter "Decide to be New in an Old Place." Before packing the car and returning home, write a letter to yourself, as if to your best friend, telling her what you discovered during your weekend away; see pages 206–7. Address the letter to yourself, and plan to mail it to yourself in a month. It will serve as a reminder that it is time for another retreat and further self-exploration.

Remember, *you are as unfinished as the shoreline along the beach, meant to transcend yourself again and again. Change takes time. You emerge slowly when you truly listen to your heart. There is no putting a time frame on soul work. May you be forever changed!*

RETREAT

Ebbing can be a rest time, a "psychic slumber" after a lifetime of learning how to be a woman.

Sink into a seamless world of uninterrupted time, where the endless hours allow something to grow from nothing.

REPAIR

I've come to despise being called strong, being the one everyone counts on to pick up the slack.

Having drifted off course, we have no choice but to find our way back, on our own. There are no lifeguards, no inner tubes to save us—inner strength and will are our lifelines.

RETRIEVE

Of primary importance for me now is to retrieve the buried parts of myself—qualities like playfulness, vulnerability, being at home in my skin, using more of my instincts. Like so many pieces of a puzzle, I need to find a way to create the whole once again.

I am no longer some hothouse flower forced into bloom, but rather a ripened woman who is getting to know what she is about.

REGROUP

Stay with your intentions—which in Latin is intendere, *meaning "to stretch toward something"—and continue to follow your instincts and intuitions.*

Just as I was finding various pieces on the beach with which to create the perfect mermaid, so must we dedicate as much time to carefully putting together the pieces of our own lives. We are all as malleable as the mermaid in the sand—unfinished men and women making new creations out of our own selves.

REGENERATE

The French woman's role is to please others, but to make sure she pleases herself in the process. I need to give my body a mind of its own—to lift the restrictions I have placed on it—to try for once to treat it as if it were all right and normal, whatever that may be.

I am learning to sponsor myself—no longer the servant but the master of my own time and destiny. It's all about the intention—knowing when to open the door and then when to close it again.

RETURN

To let myself be carried, to yield to unseen currents and be made to drift, is my primary challenge now.

Perhaps we should cheer the loss of control, our failed attempts to change others, and focus only on changing ourselves.